With best wishes

Fred. Pennington

SPECIAL MESSAGE TO READERS

This book is published under the auspices of

THE ULVERSCROFT FOUNDATION

(registered charity No. 264873 UK)

Established in 1972 to provide funds for research, diagnosis and treatment of eye diseases. Examples of contributions made are: —

A Children's Assessment Unit at Moorfield's Hospital, London.

•

Twin operating theatres at the Western Ophthalmic Hospital, London.

•

A Chair of Ophthalmology at the Royal Australian College of Ophthalmologists.

•

The Ulverscroft Children's Eye Unit at the Great Ormond Street Hospital For Sick Children, London.

You can help further the work of the Foundation by making a donation or leaving a legacy. Every contribution, no matter how small, is received with gratitude. Please write for details to:

THE ULVERSCROFT FOUNDATION,
The Green, Bradgate Road, Anstey,
Leicester LE7 7FU, England.
Telephone: (0116) 236 4325

In Australia write to:

THE ULVERSCROFT FOUNDATION,
c/o The Royal Australian College of Ophthalmologists,
27, Commonwealth Street, Sydney,
N.S.W. 2010.

FROM PLOUGHBOY TO PRIEST

Fred Pennington was reared on a remote Devon farm, where he worked with his parents to secure a hard-earned living. In this account of his interesting life he describes how primitive and basic farming was in those days. During those years he learnt duty towards his neighbour, and the value of friendship and loyalty. These experiences convinced him of the Divine purpose of God's will, and he became a parish priest, hypnotherapist and exorcist. He was inspired to use his exceptional skills to perform miracles, healing and helping people with both mental and physical ailments.

FRED PENNINGTON

FROM PLOUGHBOY TO PRIEST

Complete and Unabridged

ULVERSCROFT
Leicester

First published in Great Britain in 1984

First Large Print Edition
published 2000

British Library CIP Data

Pennington, Fred, *1911* –
From ploughboy to priest.—Large print ed.—
Ulverscroft large print series: general fiction
1. Pennington, Fred, *1911* –
2. Church of England—Clergy—Biography
3. Large type books
I. Title
283.4′2′092

ISBN 0–7089–4237–7

Published by
F. A. Thorpe (Publishing)
Anstey, Leicestershire

Set by Words & Graphics Ltd.
Anstey, Leicestershire
Printed and bound in Great Britain by
T. J. International Ltd., Padstow, Cornwall

This book is printed on acid-free paper

This book is dedicated in gratitude to my dear ones who nourished and sustained me when young. To those who taught me and guided my thoughts. To Paul Bush, who encouraged me to write this book. To all whose lives have touched mine and influenced me for good, and especially to Dorothy, without whose love and unfailing support, my life would have been so much poorer.

I welcome this opportunity to pay a tribute to Fred Pennington, author of this remarkable account of his interesting life. It is written with great sincerity of feeling; dealing with the problems that he had to face and those of the many people he has helped; expressing an intimate understanding inspired by God's love.

He recounts in fascinating detail the life and language of a remote Devon farm, situated on the Hartland Abbey estate. Here he was reared, and worked with his parents to secure a hard earned living fifty years ago. The modern generation will scarcely comprehend how primitive and basic life was on a farm in those days. All the work was done by manual labour and horse. This story contrasts the amazing changes that have occurred in a lifetime. The great agricultural depression overshadowed all rural life; hours of work were long and rewards were small.

He describes how during those years his character developed; he learnt his duty towards his neighbour, the value of friendship and loyalty, and was fortunate in finding the splendid companionship of a good wife. These experiences convinced him of the

Divine purpose of God's will.

This is a moving account of how he matured from a ploughboy to become a parish priest, hypnotherapist and exorcist. There are remarkable descriptions of his intervention and help on behalf of distressed and perplexed people, who needed understanding and guidance. It is said that faith can move mountains; Fred Pennington was certainly inspired to use the exceptional skills with which he was endowed to perform miracles, healing and helping both mental and physical ailments. His faith in God's guidance is the strength of his ministry.

Dennis Stucley

Hartland Abbey
June 1982

It is with much regret that I have to record the death of Sir Dennis Stucley a year after writing the above foreword. I wish to express my gratitude for his great interest in this book and my thanks for our life-long friendship.

F.W.P.

Part One

1

Where It All Began

'Fred! Tom! It is time to get out.' I was to hear those words many times in the years that followed: it was 7 am on January 4th, 1927 — my first day at work. I had had my fifteenth birthday the previous August and my grandmother was calling from the foot of the stairs to tell us that it was time to start work. Tom was a cousin who was ten years older than I. He had been brought up by my grandparents after his mother's death and he lived on the family farm along with my parents and younger brother.

My family have lived in the lovely parish of Hartland, North Devon, since 1550. When making a 'family tree' I discovered the earliest entry for the Pennington family in the church registers to be the burial of a sojourner, obviously a member of the family who had moved into that parish from another part of the country. An interesting fact about that 'tree' is that during those 360 years to 1910, no male member of the family had gone outside the parish to find a bride. In that year my father had brought East Anglian blood into our Devonian heritage when he married my mother from Essex.

I consider myself wonderfully blessed to have been born in such a beautiful part of the world. Hartland is a parish of some 17,000 acres, bordered on the west by the Atlantic Ocean and on the north by the Bristol Channel. In latter years it has become a Mecca for holidaymakers who find peace and tranquillity in the many coves along its shores. There are eight such coves, each with a wooded valley or combe running down from the high land on the eastern boundary of the parish, which rises to some 750 feet.

Of these valleys or 'delightful glens' as he called them, Charles Kingsley had this to say

> Each is like the other and each is like no other English scenery. Each has its upright walls, inland of rich oak-wood, nearer the sea of dark green furze, then of smooth turf, then of weird black cliffs which range out right and left far into the deep sea, in castles, spires and wings of jagged ironstone. Each has its narrow strip of fertile meadow, its crystal trout stream winding across and across from one foot-hill to another; its grey stone mill, with the water sparkling and

humming round the dripping wheel; its dark rock pools above the tide mark, where the salmon trout gather in from their Atlantic wanderings, after each Autumn flood; its ridge of blown sand, bright with golden trefoil and crimson lady's fingers; its grey banks of polished pebbles down which the stream rattles to the sea below. Each has its black field of jagged shark's tooth rock which paves the cove from side to side, streaked here and there with a pink line of shell sand, and laced with white foam from the eternal surge, stretching in parallel lines out to the westward, in strata set upright on edge, or tilted towards each other at strange angles by primitive earthquakes; such is the 'Mouth' as these coves are called, and such the jaw of teeth which they display, one rasp of which would grind abroad the timbers of the stoutest ship. To landward, all richness, softness and peace; to seaward, a waste of howling wilderness of rock and roller, barren to the fishermen, and hopeless to the shipwrecked mariner.

I think Kingsley could only have known Hartland in the storms of winter, and so missed the most wonderful exhibition of

Nature's art, the ever changing beauty of a great variety of trees, strong and well grown to the east, but stunted and leaning away from the west as one gets nearer the sea where the raging Atlantic gales sweep in to check their growth.

The variety and size of ferns in these valleys is a very beautiful sight; the shade in summer and the mild weather of winter creates a breathtaking scene. This kind of climate has its effect, too, upon the floral population. Flowers can be found at any time of the year. I remember as a lad of about ten years old being asked by our schoolmaster to collect as many kinds of wild flowers as we could find on the first day of January of that particular year, and one of my friends, Joan Wilton, was able to find 60 varieties.

Down each of these beautiful valleys there twists and turns a stream whose music is ever changing until it finally cascades over the cliff to become lost in the vastness of the ocean. One such waterfall at Speke's Mill drops in three stages, the longest of which is some 54 feet. But it is not only the waterfalls that attract one's attention along this coast: the formation of the cliffs themselves is something that has to be seen to be believed. Here can be seen the result of Nature's work over millions of years. Great upheavals of the earth's crust as if squeezed by some invisible hand, shaping the rocks into huge, cave-like structures. Kingsley said of these

> There must have been strange work here, when all these were being pressed and squeezed together like a ream of wet paper between the rival granite pincers of Dartmoor and Lundy.

It was here, then, in this beautiful corner of England, once called 'the unknown corner of England' that I first saw light of day, and where my roots are more than four centuries deep: 'the fine land, the west land, the land where I belong', or as Rudyard Kipling put it

> God gave all men all earth to love,
> And since our hearts are small,
> Ordained for each, one spot should
> prove
> Beloved over all.

2

Early Days at School

I was born on August 4th, 1911 in a little thatched cottage in the hamlet of Stoke. It was here that my father's parents lived, my grandfather having been the farm bailiff on the Hartland Abbey estate for many years. My father had left Hartland in 1904 after serving his apprenticeship in the Abbey gardens under that great gardener Gilbert Sleep, who continued in control there until the end of the First World War.

My father first went to work in Cheshire and then at Bagshot Park in Surrey, the home of the Duke of Connaught, where 120 men were employed in the gardens at that time. Here he became head gardener and while in that position he made the bouquets for the wedding of Lady Patricia Ramsey, daughter of the Duke of Connaught, to the Crown Prince of Sweden. From there he moved to a similar position at Wantage Hall in Berkshire, where he eventually met my mother.

Most of the unmarried men who worked in large gardens in those days lived in what were called 'bothies'. These were single rooms with a common kitchen where each man provided for himself and the most common utensil was the frying pan. The result of this over-indulgence in fatty foods, combined with long hours in the heat of glass-houses, brought about duodenal ulcers and because of this he decided to abandon his career as a gardener and return to his native Hartland, where he and my mother were married on September 9th, 1910. Some five months later the owner of the Abbey estate, Sir Lewis Stucley, died while on holiday in the South of France, and my grandfather was offered the tenancy of one of the farms. This was called 'Newton' and was situated one mile south of Stoke, and the same distance west of the village of Hartland.

We moved to our new home, where I was to live for the next 27 years, on Lady Day 1912. It was a much neglected farm at that time, but it had a nice large house in a good state of repair, and a range of buildings capable of housing all the stock necessary to run a farm of about 100 acres. My first memory of this house is of the morning sun shining in the window of the bedroom I shared with my brother who was two years my junior. This memory takes me back to the summer before I started school, and I have often been reminded of it when coming across Thomas Hood's poem

> I remember, I remember the house
>   where I was born,
> The little window where the sun came
>   peeping in at morn.
> He never came a wink too soon, nor
>   brought too long a day . . .

Starting school in those days was a difficult experience. Up to that time children did not come into contact with many people outside their family circle; only a few from neighbouring farms. I well remember hiding behind my mother whenever a stranger came to our house. So to be torn away suddenly one morning from the only people one had ever known, and to find oneself among some 100 or so strange and sometimes rough children at what seemed like many miles from home, was indeed a frightening experience for a five-year-old boy whose opportunities for making relationships had been so limited. How different today when children are gradually introduced to school from the age of four, and by six years of age are as self-confident as I was at ten.

After the first day, I decided that I would have none of this school business. I was taken there by a cousin who lived at the next farm to ours and our journey took us through lovely woods, which in winter turned into a very wet and muddy walk. Just before reaching the school in the village I would slip away from my escort and head for home. I did not go back to the farm at once, but waited until it was too late for my mother to take me back to school that day. But this plan worked for only two days, and one morning my mother saw me looking through the bars of the farmyard gate a full hour after I should have been in school. When I saw her coming towards me wearing her hat and coat, I knew I had to submit. She marched me back to school, opened the classroom door and pushed me in. She then went home, weeping as she went, she later told me.

It had the required effect, although the reception I had from the headmistress of the Infants' Department was far from welcoming. I can hear her now shouting at me: 'Stop that noise! Stop that noise!' But the strange thing is that from that day on I did not mind going to school at all. In fact within a short time I was enjoying the life and continued to do so to the time I left.

At that time the school took children up to the age of fourteen years, and all of them had to walk to school — some as much as four miles — from the age of five. They would leave home in the dark winter months to climb the steep cliff roads in howling south-westerly gales, and not get back until after dark.

In comparison with modern standards the conditions in the school were primitive. There was only one small water-heated radiator in each room, and in the winter we were often very cold. We had to bring packed dinners which we carried in canvas bags slung across our shoulders on the way to school; by the time we reached the school on a rainy morning, our dinners were well soaked with water. Our food had to be eaten while standing around a radiator in the cloakroom, if we were strong enough to get near it, and the meal washed down with cold water. But I cannot remember anyone ever complaining; we accepted it as being the norm. I was fortunate in that I had an aunt who lived in the village and I sometimes went there to have my dinner: we always called the midday meal 'dinner' not 'lunch', as is still the custom among the farming communities in Devon. Lunch is the snack eaten at about 10.30 am.

I started school just before the headmaster was due to retire. Mr Wilton had been head of the school for forty-three years, first of the old school, in what is now known as the Women's Institute Room, in 1874, and later of the present school when it was built in 1880. He was a firm disciplinarian, but a very kindly man who really gave himself to his teaching. Mrs Hayward, the head of the Infants Department, was also very firm and inclined to be quick tempered, especially with the very young children — a fact that some of us soon learnt to our cost. Her three-foot-long cane seemed to be ever at the ready, and when applied never failed to leave its mark!

The man who did more for me than any other teacher I had at Hartland school was Mr R. G. Bevan. He followed Mr Wilton as headmaster, and with his wife, who also taught at the school, made a deep and lasting impression on the lives of the children over many years. Our education was of a very formal nature based almost entirely on the 'three Rs', and with very few material aids other that pens and paper. Occasionally a child on reaching the age of eleven would be thought bright enough to go to the grammar school at Bideford. But they did not always do this even if educationally able. If the child's parents were farmers it was very unlikely a boy would go; he was needed on the farm as soon as he reached the age of fourteen. It was said of boys who went for higher education that they would never make good farmers because of their involvement in sport, and being away from the farm environment for five or six years, they tended to dislike heavy manual work which was the normal life on the farm.

In those days it was very rare to have a boy or girl at the school who had not been born in Hartland or a neighbouring parish. Consequently, we all spoke in our Devon dialect, even in school, and it was often the case that we found it difficult to make ourselves understood to outsiders, or even to our teachers.

From the age of five we went to school wearing heavy hobnailed boots which had to be cleaned on Saturday nights in order that they could be worn to church and Sunday school the following day. Girls always wore pinafores which, on Monday mornings, would be gleaming white and spotless. We had what was known as 'drill' each morning before starting lessons. This was something I could not understand: why, after walking four miles to school, it was thought necessary for us to spend half an hour at what is now known as P.E.

A very common breakfast before going to school in those days was known as 'kettle broth'. This was made by breaking a slice of bread into a basin, adding a lump of butter, pepper and salt, and pouring boiling water on to the bread. We often had this before going to bed, too, if we had a cold. On my way to school each day I used to call for a friend named Wilfred Mugford; he was a grandson of Jim Peard who worked for us and lived at our little cottage, 'St Leonards'. Every morning on going into his home I would find Wilfred seated at the table struggling to get through a huge basin of kettle broth, with his grandmother standing over him to make sure that he ate it all. Day after day that poor lad had a similar breakfast, which he spent so long eating that we often had to run to school to avoid being late. I well remember him commenting that when he left school he would not touch kettle broth for the rest of his life.

The games we played were very simple, mainly marbles. These games took two forms: on the way to and from school we played what was known as 'followers on'. One boy would throw a marble along the road as far as he could and still keep it in sight, while a second boy tried to get his marbles as near to that of the first boy as possible so that he could 'span' the two marbles. This meant touching one marble with his thumb and at the same time with the little finger of the same hand attempting to touch the second. If successful he could then claim his opponent's marble.

The second game was played in the playground; a marble was thrown against the wall so that it rebounded a few feet away. A second boy repeated the exercise and tried to get his marble close enough to the first to be able to span it — when he did the marble was his. In this way some boys built up quite a collection of marbles, and to us our collections seemed very valuable. One boy called Stan had such a wide span that he always seemed to win everybody else's marbles. There was always, too, the boy who dealt in marbles and seemed to make a good profit out of them. We could rarely afford to buy them even though they cost only one penny for about twenty. Some boys would try to cheat by baking their marbles in an oven, so making them rebound more sharply from the stone, giving greater accuracy. These were called 'stoneys' and there was always a careful examination of the marbles to be used before each game began.

Another game the elder boys played was called 'cats and dogs'. It was something like modern baseball except that instead of a ball, a piece of wood about six or seven inches long and an inch in diameter was 'pitched' to a boy holding a heavy stick some three feet long, and when the piece was struck it would spin at a terrific rate. This game was banned after a boy suffered a damaged eye and lost his sight. Looking back, it seems amazing that such an accident had not happened earlier in such a dangerous game, but in those days, no sports equipment was provided by the school, so we had to improvise our own games.

Another very popular pastime we called 'fox and hounds'. This we played after dinner, before afternoon school. One boy would set off across the fields and after about ten minutes or so a dozen of the more energetic ones would give chase, shouting, 'eek, squeak, whistle or ollee [holler], else the little dug want vollee [dog won't follow]'. This sometimes took up to two hours and we did not get back to school that day, which inevitably meant trouble the following day, rewarded either by the cane or by being kept in after school; we were sometimes kept in for up to an hour while the teacher marked papers. Whenever possible we arranged the 'hunt' to take place on a Friday, hoping that the teacher would forget the incident by the following Monday.

Some of the games we played would be thought very childish today. Hoops, for instance, were very popular up to the time we left school at fourteen. These were made of half-inch iron, some three feet in diameter, by one of the two local blacksmiths, Stan Dayman or George Beardmore. The hoops were propelled by what we called a 'skimmer', a piece of metal about three feet in length with a loop at one end, by which we held the skimmer and pushed the hoop along at a terrific speed. Looking back to those days I often wonder where we got all our energy from, most of our games being of a very boisterous nature.

At the age of ten, we were given by our headmaster the names and addresses of children in various parts of what was then the British Empire, to correspond with as pen-pals. My pal was the son of a farmer who lived in Western Australia and farmed three thousand acres. We used to exchange photographs and pressed flowers and write to each other about our school life; later we shared our farming experiences. More than 60 years later, we still correspond. Although we have never met, we feel as if we know each other as well as if we had been brought up together. It seems I know his farm and that part of Australia as well as if I had lived there.

A familiar sight as we walked through the village to school each morning was that of Alf Jeffery delivering milk. This he did from two buckets, slung on either side of a yoke across his shoulders. The milk was put into jugs and other containers left on the doorsteps, by means of a long-handled half-pint measure. I often used to wonder how long those jugs were left lying outside the doors, and if any dogs or cats helped themselves.

Alf was also a 'colt breaker'. This meant that he trained young shire horses of about two or three years of age. First he got the colt used to having a bit in its mouth, then he walked it round and round for hours, until it responded to the rein properly. The next move was to put the horse in chains, that is, to pull a heavy log of wood with chains fastened to a neck collar. When the colt became used to the feel of the chains on its sides, and the weight of the load on its shoulders, it was made to pull various types of implements alongside an older and more stable horse.

The final part of the young horse's training was to be put between shafts to learn how to pull carts and other farm vehicles. This was done by putting the youngster into what was known as a 'brake', a very heavy, strong type of dog-cart, which the colt could not destroy, or cause injury to itself if it began to kick or become frightened in any way. Alf and his brake was often seen on the roads around our village, gently but firmly coaxing his young charge to walk down the road in a straight line. From a very early age we were taught to stand perfectly still by the roadside whenever we met Alf and his colt, so that we would not frighten the young animal in any way.

Like most boys, I loved bird-nesting, but mine took on a rather more dangerous form than that in which most boys indulged. My friends and I searched for birds' eggs on the cliffs and rocks of our coast, and when I look now at some of the places we used to climb on those 300-foot-high cliffs, my hair almost stands on end. But the birds that fascinated me most were the swallows that came year after year to the same nests under the eaves of our barn. Then there were the house martins which built their nests in the lofts of the cattle sheds. They all seemed to be a part of our family when they arrived to spend each summer with us.

A pastime at which we spent many happy hours as small boys was 'tickling' trout. On our way home from school we walked for about half a mile through a beautiful valley which had a stream that abounded with trout. We caught the fish by very gently turning up a large stone under which a trout was hiding, quietly passing a very fine loop of wire over its tail and jerking it out of the water. I have caught many a nice breakfast in this way, but I'm afraid the close season was something quite unknown to us.

We had very little pocket money when we were young; for most of us it was one penny each Monday morning, but often there would be a farthing left over at the end of that week. The little sweet shops belonging to Maudie Bond and Mrs Ware were our favourite haunts. There we could get four 'gob-stoppers' for a farthing, or six long strips of liquorice at the same cost.

One of the highlights of our life in those days was the Hartland Cottage Garden Show. This was started in 1857, and has been held on the last Wednesday of July each year since that date, apart from the war years. The day began with a parade of the children led by the Town Band through the village to the Market Field where a huge marquee was set up, providing the most wonderful display of vegetables, flowers and fruit, as well as an exhibition of dressmaking, cookery, flower arrangements and childrens' competitions which had been arranged and judged during the morning. On arriving at the field we all made a mad rush for the tent to see who had won the various competitions. There were some great gardeners in Hartland in those days, and I was always amazed at the high quality of the produce shown by men like Charlie Dayman, Harry Shute, Tom Prouse and brothers Jim and Joe Heywood, and so many others year after year, and amazed too by the amount of work they must have put into their gardens. I remember seeing them working in those same gardens during the spring and early summer after doing a hard day's work of nine and a half hours on a farm, and then spending the whole evening in their garden until it became too dark to see what they were doing.

They must have spent many hours, too, in preparing their produce for the exhibition. The potatoes had to be scrubbed and chosen for quality and evenness of size; the beans and peas needed to be of equal length and quality, but all their labour seemed well worth while when the judges placed that blue card beside their exhibit. Some of these men used to have as many as thirty entries in the various classes. The ladies, too, were not to be outdone. Their entries of homemade bread, cakes, chutneys and pickles, and their efforts in dressmaking and knitting were quite outstanding — the result of many hours of painstaking work.

After the presentation of the cups and trophies we all moved into the next field where a sports programme had been arranged which went on until eight-thirty in the evening, with a break of an hour for tea in the Palladium — a small nissen hut type of building where most of the social events took place. Here again there was very keen competition, especially in the open races, when people from other parishes took part. Jack Bragg and Ned Heard seemed to run neck and neck each year. Then there was little Tommy Hockin whom no one could catch in the long distance races; and Bill Gifford from Morwenstowe inevitably won all the cycle speed races, even though he had only one arm.

It was a great day for us children because apart from the few pence we won at the sports, we were usually given an extra sixpence or so by our parents to spend at Mrs O'Donnell's ice-cream stall, where we could buy mazzards, locally grown fruit shaped like small very sweet plums which have now become almost extinct — I have memories of many mazzard-daubed faces on Garden Show Day.

The final jollifications of the day would begin promptly at nine o'clock in the Palladium. This was a dance which lasted until two in the morning. The veleta, the waltz, the barn dance and the quadrilles, as well as such innovations as the foxtrot, the quick step and the Charleston, were all indulged, with hardly room to move. The singing of 'God Save the King' would bring to an end a great day in our lives, and we would then sleepily wend our way home through the dark woods, with the path pin-pointed by myriads of glow-worms, and across the little wooden bridge we used each day on our way to and from school. The only sound would be the occasional hoot of an owl, or a rabbit scurrying away into the undergrowth at the sight of our oil lantern. Foremost in our thoughts at the end of each Garden Show would be the fact that two days hence we would 'break up' from school for the long summer holiday of four weeks.

3

Becoming a Farmer's Boy

For those of us brought up on a farm, school holidays usually meant hard work from an early age. I started school in the middle of the First World War, when many young men who worked on the land were conscripted into the army. Consequently labour was very scarce during those years, and many farmers had some of their horses commandeered, adding to the labour problem.

Not only were horses taken in this way, but hay as well. Some city-bred man would arrive at a farm without warning, saying that the authorities wanted this or that rick of hay. He would then make an estimate of the number of tons in a particular rick into which he put an iron bar with WD in large letters at one end, and a barb at the other, which prevented the bar from being removed before the hay was taken away by a War Department lorry.

I remember, sometime in 1916, a very 'cocky' little character arriving at our farm demanding to be shown our ricks of hay. My father did as he was ordered, after which the official espied a rick which had not been pointed out to him because it was of rushes, cut during the summer months and used as winter bedding for the cattle. To our astonishment he promptly stuck a WD bar into this rick also, and after measuring it, announced that we should be paid for so many tons of hay. Naturally my father protested, saying that this rick did not contain anything fit for horses to eat, only rushes. The little man simply made a joke of these protests, saying that my father should pull the other leg also. Eventually a cheque arrived in payment for so many tons of hay.

Another example of waste which occurred on many farms during that war, was the fact that after the rick of hay had been commandeered and stamped with the War Department bar, it was never claimed, even though the farmers had received their cheques. Those ricks remained, in some cases for three or four years until the war ended, and were eventually used by the farmer.

From an early age I had learnt to milk cows — so early in fact, that I cannot remember my first attempt. This meant that I had to milk two cows before going to school each morning. One of these — and they were always the quietest — was a cow called Granny. She was the only Guernsey we kept and was kept to increase the butterfat content of the milk from the other ten or twelve cows. Granny lived to a great age, and I never knew her to become agitated or upset.

From as far back as I can remember farm animals have been a very real part of my life. I grew up surrounded by them and lived day by day in close contact with them. I knew each of them individually: their family tree, their character and their little whims and fancies.

The dogs were among my earliest animal friends. I was very fond of Abbess, a collie/Old English sheepdog cross, who was my constant companion before I started school. She was a very intelligent animal who seemed to know me so well and anticipated my every move. I remember my parents telling me that one day when I was three years old they suddenly realised that I was no longer around the farmyard, and that Abbess, too, was missing. A search party was organised, and eventually I was found some two miles from home, with Abbess walking sedately in front of me. When asked where I was going, I replied: 'I'm going to Bideford to see my Aunty Poll.' Bideford was about fourteen miles away, but at least Abbess was leading me in the right direction.

Soon after I started school my beloved

doggie pal died in her sleep, but one of her puppies, whom we called Nun, soon took her place in my affections. She, too, was a most faithful creature, and on looking over some old photographs of those days, Nun seems always to have been with me. The dogs never came into the house alone; they would lie for hours on a mat in the porch with the door wide open and never attempt to come inside. At night they slept on a bundle of straw in the warmth of the stable. These dogs had a wonderful understanding of their work. They had to help with both the cattle and the sheep, and they seemed to know just how much pressure to put on each group. With the sheep they were very gentle, never frightening them nor causing the in-lamb ewes to hurry, but when they had to fetch or drive cattle, one would not think they were the same dogs; they would even nip the heels of any particularly difficult bullock.

When the sheep were dipped each year at the end of July or early August, it was the custom of the farmer to put the sheepdogs through the dipping tank after finishing the sheep; it was thought that any fleas would be destroyed in this way. I did not like this custom at all and as a boy just before the last sheep was put through the trough, I would quietly slip away with Nun.

Every animal kept on the farm in those days seemed to serve a useful purpose, and no animal was kept as a pet only. Even the cats were not allowed in the house, despite being well fed and cared for, in order that they would destroy the rats and mice around the corn ricks and cattle sheds.

One of the first jobs I can remember being given to do on the farm was to take lunch and 'drinking' out to the men in the harvest fields. Lunch was at about 10.30 am when we generally had bread and cheese and a jug of tea; 'drinking' was a sort of high tea at 5 pm when there were pasties of potato, egg and meat as well as many other good things. The food would be eaten sitting on the hay or sheaves of corn. When it got dark and the men couldn't see to work any longer, everyone came in and sat down to a supper of cold meat and boiled potatoes, washed down with cider.

As I grew older, another job that came my way was leading a horse — generally our little New Forest pony called Polly — when we 'scarified' the root crops of mangolds, turnips and potatoes. This meant leading Polly up and down the rows while someone, usually my cousin Tom, held the scarifier. This implement had a wheel in the front and three blades at the back, which cut under the weeds between the rows of the root crops. This job had to be done every two weeks or so in the late spring and summer, especially when the weather was wet and the weeds grew quickly. Another 'boy's job' as it was called, was to lead the horse in the wagon when loading hay or corn.

In the winter, with the cattle lying in, there was always plenty for a boy to do, fetching and carrying hay and straw around the cattle sheds. The one job I disliked more than any other was picking up stones in grass fields where hay was going to be cut. If not picked up these stones would damage the blades of the mowing machine. Stone picking was done in early May with a horse and 'butt', a two-wheeled cart with enclosed sides and ends — one of the most common means of transport on farms in those days. We slowly worked our way across each field, each covering a strip of about five yards, in a to-and-fro movement, until the whole field had been covered.

When we were quite young we used to imitate our elders, by trying to do the same work as they were doing. For instance, at mangold pulling time, while the men were carrying in the roots with a horse and butt, we would take one of the sheepdogs, usually my faithful Nun, and with a harness of rope she would pull a box on wheels full of mangolds from the field to the yard. She seemed to enjoy the fun as much as we did.

Threshing day was always an exciting time. This usually took place in winter, when we used to have three or four such days at intervals of a month or six weeks and when we children managed to have the day off from school each time. The threshing machine would be brought into the 'mooey' or rick-yard and pulled up alongside a rick of corn. Quite often it would not get to us until almost midnight, having threshed at another farm until quite late.

The machine was drawn along the roads by a twin-cylinder Burrell steam engine. This was a magnificent machine with gleaming brasses and wheels that were over six feet high which was the envy of every schoolboy. It was driven along the roads at about four miles an hour with two men on the engine — one at the controls and one steering — while a third man was compelled by law to walk in front with a red flag. 'Diddle' Harris was the driver and Jack Nicholls did the steering; the 'third man', as he was called, was 'Artful' Prouse.

These men had no transport to get to and from their homes, and often they would have to walk up to four miles after bringing the machine to a farm late at night, and another four back in the morning to be there by 7 am to light the boiler and get up steam ready for threshing to begin at about 8.30 am. Everyone involved was provided with all their meals on threshing days — and what wonderful meals they were — from breakfast at 7.30 am to supper when the day's threshing was finished. There always seemed to be such joy at those meals, especially in the evening with twelve or fourteen men really enjoying their food after a hard and often dusty day. I remember once sitting at the supper table when I felt a tickle on my neck, and there sat a mouse on my shoulder, looking up into my face as if wondering what it was all about; it had obviously crawled up my trousers during the day while I was working on the corn rick.

These three machine men often worked under intolerable conditions. The corn was nearly always dusty, and when it had been carried from the field in an unfit condition, and had become 'yetted' or heated in the rick, the 'stewer', as we called the dust, was so bad that the men working near the machine could barely be seen. They were enveloped in a cloud of thick dust day after day, especially the man who looked after the bundles of straw as they came from the machine. Many of these men eventually contracted 'farmer's lung', which is not surprising when one realises they worked in these conditions for more than six months every year. But even these conditions were not as bad when the threshing had to be done in the confined space of a barn, before portable engines became available. I can just remember such times, the threshing usually being done in the evenings, after a day's work outside. The dust then was indescribable.

There was something wonderful about a threshing day: the hum of the machine and the sight of the corn pouring into the bags which were emptied into an ever-growing heap in the granary seemed a more than adequate reward for all the hard work that had gone into its production. It gave me an overpowering feeling of gratitude. As a small boy I used to love to go into the 'mooey' in the quiet of the evening, when the machines and men had gone; after the noise and bustle of the day, there was a wonderful peace. That lovely rick of corn that had stood there in the early morning, with its thatch all neatly trimmed, had gone. All that was left was a rick of straw, a heap of 'douse' and a pile of 'riddlings'. 'Douse' were the husks that had surrounded the corn in the ear, and which had been blown out by the machine; in the case of oats these were soft and sweet and much loved by the cattle. 'Riddlings' were the broken pieces of straw, too short to be tied into bundles, which were used as bedding for the cattle. I would climb the steps up to the granary and feast my eyes upon the great heap of corn smelling so sweet and wholesome; the result of many hours of labour and sunshine and rain.

When wheat had been threshed, two or three bags were taken to the mill to be ground into flour. All the flour we used in those days was from our home-grown wheat. Tom Fulford was the miller and he always seemed to be covered in flour whenever I saw him; I often wondered if he went to bed in that state, but I'm sure he didn't. I can still hear the roar of the water from the leat dropping on to the mill-wheel and the hum of the millstones as they ground the wheat into the flour. The bran and offals were separated, bagged and loaded along with the flour into the cart to be taken back to the farm. The flour was kept in the kitchen in what was known as the 'flour hutch', and what lovely flour it was — absolutely pure and wholesome. The bran was kept for sick horses and cattle who suffered digestive problems during the winter when they were kept indoors on dry foods. A bran mash for a day or so generally cured them.

The roads in those days were very rough indeed. The stones used for their repair were dug in local quarries and hauled by horse and butt and left in heaps beside the road where they were needed. There they were 'cracked' as we termed it, into small pieces the size of a golfball, by men using metal hammers. These men were called stone breakers — two who worked near our farm were Bill Mugford and Fred Rowland. The latter had a son, also called Fred, who was one of my closest pals at school. He had a wonderful brain and was always far ahead of any of us in our class. Fred could have reached great heights in the academic world, but like most of us at that time, he had to work with his father on leaving school, breaking stones. It was hard and often dangerous work, for which they were paid 15 pence in old money for each cubic yard. The broken stones were spread on the roads and covered with earth, then they were sprayed with water and rolled in by a heavy steam roller until the mixture formed an even surface.

4

Memories of Hartland Abbey and Early Church-going

During my early years, my grandfather still had close connections with Hartland Abbey, and I often went with him when he visited Lady Marion Stucley. I was always intrigued by the men working in the saw-pit on the estate. This was where all the wood for building and repairs was sawn into the required sizes by hand. The pit was some six feet long, three wide and six deep. The trunk of the tree to be sawn was laid across the width of the pit, in which one man stood to pull the saw downwards, while a man above pulled it upwards. The saw used for this purpose had teeth which all faced in one direction, so that it cut on the downward stroke. This was extremly hard work for the man beneath who continually had the sawdust in his eyes, and the men changed places at frequent intervals. Bill Webber, whom I later came to know well, worked in that saw-pit for many years, as had my grandfather in his young days.

The Abbey park contained a herd of some fifty fallow deer at that time, and I used to watch Keeper Colwill stalking stags to shoot from time to time, both to control their numbers and for the venison. They were beautiful creatures; we often stumbled across a fawn lying hidden in the bracken during the early summer.

In the grounds of the Abbey there were many peacocks strutting around showing off their beautiful plumage. The cry of the peahen is one of the first sounds I can remember, and when I hear it now, I am at once transported back to my boyhood days.

Lady Stucley gave a party for the schoolchildren at the Abbey each Christmas and we often became lost there in the maze of corridors and passages. I have come to know that lovely old house intimately since those days, but as a boy I almost expected to meet a monk dressed in his habit in one of those passages; I used to try to imagine myself living there in those far-off days.

Another important part of my childhood, even more important than I realised at the time, was church-going and Sunday school. We went to the parish church at Stoke, where my family had worshipped since 1550, as a family, almost every Sunday. From a very early age I knew a wonderful sense of belonging to that lovely old church — almost as if I were part of the building and had been there from its beginning.

Church-going in those days was seen as a very real part of living and almost everyone went to church, though not always perhaps for the right reason as there was still an element of Victorianism in our attitude to worship. Perhaps I am being too harsh in making that statement, because I remember marvelling at the courage and devotion shown by so many people in the face of great adversity and inconvenience in getting to church. Two men stand out as especially clear examples: Dick and Lewis Avery were brothers who lived at Fattacott, some four miles from the church, and who hardly ever failed to be in their places each Sunday morning. That walk would not have been easy in all weathers for a normally fit person, but Dick had a deformed foot and walked with the aid of a stick. They would have had to be up and about early enough to feed and tend their stock on the farm, before changing their clothes and setting off to walk to church and back again. Such sacrifices were not uncommon in those days in a farming community, in order to get to church.

There was a very real antagonism between the Anglican and Methodist churches in those days. No one would dream of going to a service in the other's church except for a funeral or on Armistice Day. In fact I well remember my grandfather warning me as a small boy never to go to the chapel because 'It is of the Devil'. Extempore prayer in the Anglican church was said to be 'chapelly', and was frowned upon. Equally any prayers read from a book in the Methodist church were said to be 'churchy, and not from the heart'. Confirmation services in the Anglican church and what were known as Revival Meetings with conversions in the Methodist church were the signal for much barracking and derisive language on both sides. But the young antagonists were the closets of friends in every other activity.

There were several special services during the year when the church would be full, with seats in the aisles. There were Patronal Festivals, Harvest Festival and what we used to call Armistice Day — Remembrance Day as it is now known.

St Nectan, the patron saint of our parish church, was probably one of a number of Celtic people who were driven out of Wales and settled in Devon and Cornwall during the period of King Arthur. Legend has it that he was the eldest child of the largest family of Brychan, a Welsh kinglet, after whom Brecknockshire is named. It is thought that he landed at Padstow along with several brothers and sisters as a missionary group, and travelled along the coast to Tintagel, where his kieve, or cell, can still be seen. Later he moved further up the coast to Hartland, leaving his sister Morwenna at what is now known as Morwenstowe. He probably set up a 'cell' or small church at Newton, the farm which was my home, previously known as Nova Villa. The remains of a church can still be seen there, called St Leonards, but it is unlikely that this was Nectan's original church. He seems to have made his headquarters here for his work of converting the heathens in the area.

Nectan was beheaded on June 17th, 520 AD in a field at Newton known as Church Park, and tradition has it that he ran, with his head under his arm, the mile to a well at Stoke, where he died. It is also recorded by tradition that one of the men who beheaded Nectan later went out of his mind, and tore his flesh and bit off his tongue with his teeth, and so died miserably. Another man, who had held the victim while he was being beheaded, at once lost his sight, but as he stumbled along the road endeavouring to follow Nectan, he touched some of his blood and his sight was restored, whereupon he glorified God.

The first known church in honour of St Nectan was built about 1060 by Gytha, wife of the great Earl Godwin, and mother of King Harold. She dedicated it to St Nectan because she believed the prayer of that saint had saved her husband from shipwreck off our dangerous coast. St Nectan's relics were carefully preserved at Stoke church, probably beneath the high altar, until they were disturbed at the reformation. It is interesting to note that a bone of this great saint is one of the most treasured relics of King Harold's church at Waltham Abbey in Essex.

St Nectan's Day was, and still is, kept on June 17th. We always had a half holiday from school to attend a service in church, after which everyone was given an unleavened biscuit bearing the seal of the patron saint. A dynamic preacher was always present at these services, and I can still remember some of their texts after more than sixty years. If the weather was good on these occasions we used to go down to one of the coves, either Blackpool Mill or Speke's Mill, for tea and games, until it grew dark. Many a teenage romance began to blossom during those walks home in the twilight hours.

Harvest Festival, too, was always a very popular and inspiring service at Hartland. The wonderful spread at the tea which followed the service always intrigued us. The tables seemed to be presided over by the same stately ladies, year after year, each with her precious silver teapot and water jug, brought out and polished for the occasion, and the tables almost groaned under the weight of so much lovely food.

On November 11th, 1919 the annual commemoration of the ending of the First World War began. On the Sunday nearest to that date all the ex-service men — about 120 in the years immediately following the war, headed by the Town Band some 26 strong, and with the schoolchildren bringing up the rear, marched to the parish church 1½ miles away for a remembrance service. In the evening we did the same at the Methodist church in the village, little thinking that we, the children, would be attending as adults 26 years later after another war: but at that time we would be remembering some of our own pals who had marched with us as children, and who had given their lives in the Second World War.

Sunday school was held in the 'chapel of ease' in the village. This small church, which had once been the Market Hall when Hartland held a weekly pannier market, had 'horse-box' pews. These were a great attraction to us as children; we could hide behind them without being seen by the vicar, Prebendary Gregory, who worked hard and long to instil in us the rudiments of the Christian faith. As small children we were taught by a Miss Prust, a lady who never seemed to age. She was of the oldest family in Hartland, records of whom go back to the fifteenth century. I am afraid the poor lady had a very difficult time trying to teach us, and one feels ashamed now at the awful tricks we played on her.

Prebendary Gregory laid a very solid foundation on which to build our Christian lives, and though I threw it all to the winds for a time, his teaching has always remained deep in my unconscious mind, and has become available to me as and when I wanted it. It never seems to have grown old, and when I have dug it out, it had been as fresh as the day he gave it to me. At the time I was being taught, I was not consciously aware of receiving anything, so much so, that when I reached the age of fifteen and went forward for confirmation, the whole thing seemed to be so meaningless, that I rejected the Christian faith completely. Looking back at those days, I realise how much I must have hurt the vicar and Sunday school teachers, because I myself now know something of that heartache.

Despite the fact that many people still believe that the places of worship were always full at every service in those days, Good Friday was certainly not well attended — at least, not by the farming community and anyone with a garden. Practically every farmer set aside that day to 'dock' his sheep, that is, to trim the wool around their hindquarters so that it shouldn't get soiled before shearing time arrived. If docking was not done at this time of the year, 'blow-flies' would lay their maggot-producing eggs, which in the days before insecticides were a real menace. The man with a garden usually spent that day making his first sowing of seeds and tilling his potatoes. I am sure that neither of these jobs had any connection with Good Friday, and why they were always done on that day I don't know. I can only assume that the day generally coincided with the growth of fresh grass which made the sheep 'scour', and for the gardener, it was his first free day since Christmas, so it was a good time to get the gardening done.

An outstanding memory of Good Friday from my very young days is of baker George Gifford coming round the farms, very early on that day, selling hot cross buns from his horse-drawn covered wagon.

5

My Home When a Boy

In my early years our home life was much closer than is the case with many families today. We had no means of transport, so we not only worked as a family, but our fun was also confined mainly to the home.

One of my earliest recollections is of bathing in the kitchen in a galvanised metal bath before a roaring open fire. In winter this fire was kept alight day and night by what we called a 'back stick', a huge log about four feet long which would still be glowing brightly when we got up in the mornings. The walls of our house were about three feet thick, and with the fireplace being some nine feet wide, we were able to sit inside it, with the lovely fire in the middle.

There, too, the 'hand-maids' were hanging; these were iron hooks slung from a bar some six feet above the fire, on which cast-iron kettles and 'crocks' were hung. These could be lowered or raised by notches on the bar, and each had a handle enabling the boiling water to be poured out without having to touch the kettle. Crocks were round, cast-iron containers holding three or four gallons of water in which meat and other things were boiled. In the corners of the chimney piece, as we called it, hams of pork were hung to smoke.

It was here, in a wonderful peace and tranquillity, that I remember spending so many happy winter evenings, with the fire roaring up the wide chimney, and the paraffin lamp glowing on the table. I used to listen enthralled to the stories my grandfather told about farming in his young days and of his life in the last century. He had a wonderful knack of using a simple story or an experience of his life to illustrate a moral or practical issue. He used to sit in a high-backed wooden chair, upholstered with horse hair, that his grandfather had made. He smoked a 'churchwarden' pipe — a clay pipe with a stem some twelve inches long, and I can still remember the smell of that strong 'shag' tobacco, and the curl of smoke wafting up the open chimney. Sometimes we played cards, a game called 'don' which was very common in those days.

One of the most fascinating stories my grandfather had to tell was how he used to be taken sometimes to the cliff top on a very dark and stormy night, where a horse was being led to and fro with a lantern tied to its side. This was to entice a ship to come in closer and so become stranded on those terrible rocks, where the cargo would be plundered.

I am afraid the inhabitants of that coast had a very bad name in the shipping world. As late as 1922, I remember a Greek ship ran aground in a very thick fog. Several of us rushed down to the beach where it had come ashore, to be confronted by the captain standing on the bridge of his ship with a revolver in his hand, defying anyone to come near. He had obviously heard of what might happen to a ship wrecked on that coast.

Hardly a winter passed, in those days, without a ship being wrecked on our beaches, during the terrible gales sweeping in from the Atlantic Ocean. There was a memorable wreck in 1934: the *Radyr*, out of Swansea and loaded with coal. Like many another vessel coming down the Bristol Channel to head out into the teeth of an Atlantic storm, she sheltered that day in Lundy roads. Lundy Island sits astride the mouth of the Bristol Channel, and offers a wonderful shelter for ships waiting for a storm to abate. That day there were some twenty vessels taking shelter, and towards evening, as we watched from the cliff top, we saw *Radyr* pull out and head for the open sea. She first had to pass through what is known as Harty Race, a ten-mile stretch of water between Lundy Island and Hartland Point. The water here is always troubled, even in fine weather, but in a severe gale it becomes very rough indeed.

Radyr seemed to negotiate that area well enough, but as she came into the open Atlantic, into mountainous seas, she became more and more engulfed. As she came abreast of us around the point, we lost sight of her for several minutes at a time. Then she would rise out of a trough, almost on her stern, only to plunge down the other side of a huge wave. When it began to get dark we had to leave and early the next morning we heard that she had disappeared, the first evidence being the body of one of her crew on Berry beach. We knew from experience that if no more bodies came in that day, we should have to wait ten days for others that might be washed ashore. We knew too, that by then they would be unidentifiable, because of those terrible rocks. There used to be a part of the churchyard set aside for the burial of unidentified bodies, which we called Strangers Hill. Today, thanks to modern means of communication and warning systems, this is no longer used, but the storms still lash the coast and Lundy

Roads is still a welcome refuge for many ships.

In my early years, all the family cooking was done in a 'cloam' oven. This was built into the side of the open fireplace, lined with fire resistant clay and closed in by an iron door. The oven was heated by 'faggots', or bundles of gorse or other small wood that burnt quickly and easily. When the fire brick became white hot, the fire and some of the ashes were raked out, and the prepared food put into bake. Baking took place once a week, and bread, cakes and pasties of all descriptions were made on that day. The flavour of food cooked in those ovens was out of this world.

A great step forward in easing the work of the cook was the introduction of the 'bodley'. This was a cooking range, burning coal or wood, which was closed up when cooking, but could be used as an open fire to warm the room at other times. It was always cleaned and polished with black-lead so that it shone like a mirror.

The lighting in our homes in those days consisted of a paraffin lamp in the main living room, and candles in the bedrooms. In our work in the stables, cattle sheds and barns, we used hurricane lanterns which we often had to hang round our necks as we carried bundles of straw and hay for the stock. They gave us light for many other jobs, such as lambing and calving. The old 'bat' lanterns as they were called, would stand up to a great deal of rough treatment as we trudged around the fields in the early hours of the morning checking sheep in a howling Atlantic gale. I never knew such a lantern to blow out. With the coming of the incandescent mantle, the lighting in our homes was much improved, in fact we wondered how we ever managed to read by the light of the old wick lamp. But there was still better to come when the pressurised lamps were introduced for use outside as well as indoors.

The furniture in our kitchen was of a very practical nature. The table was similar to those found in any farmhouse at that time: long and narrow, some three feet by ten feet, with a form on either side running its whole length. This kind of table was very necessary at that time, especially on threshing days and at hay and corn harvests, when fourteen or fifteen men came in for their meals. Each man was provided with full board during those special days, and this was considered to be part of their wages. Free cider and beer helped to make up a man's earnings to 25 shillings per week. At least a man was sure of his food, which was a real aid to his well-being, as was the land on which he grew his potatoes, along with free milk and other perks.

The floor of the kitchen was typical of those found in farmhouses, being of blue stone slabs with a mat in front of the fire. These floors may be considered cold by modern standards, but there could be no place for carpets when all kinds of animals were brought into that room to be warmed. During the lambing season, especially when the weather was bad, there were always new-born lambs to be found in the kitchen, where the womenfolk sought to bring warmth and new life into their cold little bodies with a drop of brandy. Sometimes it was a weak new-born pig, snuffling and grunting as it found new strength by the fire.

Another interesting room in our home was the dairy. Here the milk was separated and the cream made into butter. The warm milk was brought straight from the cows and put through a separator, which was turned by hand. The milk was forced through small apertures, called cups, which revolved at a great speed, so forcing the cream from the milk by centrifugal action. The left-over milk was fed to small calves being reared for beef, which reminds me of another job we did as boys: we put a hand into a bucket of milk and allowed a calf to suck our finger and so take the milk. There was always the difficult, boisterous bull calf who wanted the others' share of the milk as well as his own, and was quite prepared to barge his head into another calf's bucket, and even knock it out of your hand if you were not careful. Or the shy little heifer calf who was reluctant to suck a finger at all, but preferred the natural way of having her breakfast and supper; only when she became very hungry would she at last take the milk.

Butter was made almost every day, after the cream had been 'scalded'. This meant that a bowl of cream was put to stand in a larger bowl of water over a fire until the cream was heated to a little less than boiling point. There were no thermometers, so when the surface of the cream began to crinkle, it was taken off the fire and put in a cool window of the dairy. Each of the two types of cream produced at that time had a distinct flavour. The cream made by the method just decribed was known as separated cream, and the other type was called clotted cream. This was made by placing milk straight from the cows into shallow bowls, where it was allowed to stand for twenty-four hours, until the cream had risen to the surface. The milk was then heated to just under boiling point, until the top of the cream showed small bubbles, when it was put aside to cool. The top layer was skimmed off as Devonshire clotted cream.

Separated cream made the best-flavoured butter: this was made by whipping the cream round and round in a large wooden bowl by hand, until the cream thickened into butter. This process never ceased to fascinate me as a small boy: I would sit with my eyes fixed on that bowl of cream as my mother whipped it around, and all the while it got thicker and thicker, and changed colour from cream into a deeper yellow. The liquid remaining after the butter was made was known as buttermilk. This had the most wonderful flavour, and was a delicacy much sought after by the children; we often had it before going to bed.

The butter was next washed in cold water and kneaded to get out all the buttermilk which would otherwise impair its keeping qualities. Salt was added and the butter was washed again, after which it was weighed up into pounds and half pounds in rectangular blocks. This was done with a pair of 'Scotch-hands' — two pieces of wood about six inches by three inches with handles, one side of which was corrugated. The butter was pounded and slapped into shape with these and the individual design of the buttermaker was inscribed on the top of each block, so that the buyer would know exactly whose butter he was getting. Our butter was usually sold in the Pannier Market at Bideford, and up to twenty pounds at a time had to be carried in huge baskets the one mile to the village and then put on a horse-drawn bus belonging to William Colwill for the rest of the journey; later on it was sent by Tom Williams' motor bus. The carriage charge for each basket was two pence, and the butter was eventually sold for four pence per pound in the old days.

Butter making was not always an easy job. When the weather was very hot, and especially when it was thundery, my mother would have to get up early in the morning while it was still cool and sit beside the well from which we got all our water; she would sit and stir that cream until it became butter. It was impossible to make it while the temperature was high.

Another interesting utensil in the dairy was the 'trendle'. This was a large, oval-shaped, earthenware container, about four feet long, three wide and two deep, which was glazed inside. Twice each year we killed a pig, which was cut up into joints and salt was well rubbed into each. The joints were placed in the trendle in a brine mixture, and they remained edible for several months. As each joint was required for the table it was soaked overnight in water to remove the salt. The bacon of those days would be unrecognisable today; it was very fat and cut into thick slices. This, along with fried potatoes, was a frequent meal in my young days. If the hams were not to be smoked in the open fireplace they were 'sweet pickled'. This was done by placing the ham in a large earthenware dish, where it was basted several times a day with a mixture of vinegar, sugar and many kinds of spice and herbs. The result when cooked was the most delicious tasting ham.

One other common object in the dairy, apart from the rows and rows of home-made jams, chutneys, pickles and other preserves, were the 'steins' — earthenware containers about three feet high and one and a half feet in diameter in the middle. In these, eggs were pickled. Unlike today's hens, who spend their lives in batteries, the poultry of that time had complete freedom to roam at will and so were not forced into laying eggs in the autumn and winter as they are now. The natural tendency is for hens to lay their eggs during the spring and summer months, so there would be very few eggs in the winter and the steins were used to store surplus eggs in the summer for winter use. They kept beautifully fresh in a chemical mixture called water-glass.

The great amenities we lacked in those days were, of course, running water and indoor lavatories. Everyone, young and old, had to use an earth closet some twenty yards down the garden path. If anyone was so unfortunate as to need it in the middle of a cold winter's night, then it was very definitely a freezing experience. But no one complained, and when the closet was looked after carefully and kept clean, it was as hygienic as many modern systems.

6

The Joys of Farm Life

Such was the home in which I was brought up — a home where love and harmony prevailed. We had few of the material luxuries of life but we were content with simple things; we lived very close to nature and enjoyed the changing seasons. Farming was a way of life in those days, rather than a business. Often on a Sunday evening in summer, one or other of the neighbouring farmers would come to our farm, or we would go to theirs, and stroll around the fields, discussing the crops and livestock. All our farming friends were addressed as 'Farmer' so-and-so in those days. Perhaps we would go into a field of mangolds and someone would remark that they were not growing as well as they might. Farmer Heard might say 'Why not give them some nitre?', by which he meant nitrate of soda, and he would tell how much it had helped his crop. Next we might inspect the cattle, and someone might notice that one animal had an unhealthy coat. This would at once bring a response, perhaps from Farmer Oke: 'A dose of turpentine and Stockholm tar would be good for that one.' And so the conversation would go on all around the farm; then we would go back to the house for a cup of tea. Listening to these conversations, as a lad, I learnt a great deal about the life and work of the farmer.

I had many pets as child. Polly the pony, who I shared with my brother, was a source of great joy to me; in fact we grew up together, being of the same age. She came to us when I was two years old. Of all the animals with which I ever had contact, I think Polly was the most 'human'. She seemed at times almost to read my thoughts, and she certainly anticipated my actions. She was a most gentle creature with whom I spent so many happy hours, both at work and at play. I never went hunting with Polly, because that sport never appealed to me, even though I was brought up and lived with the sound of the hunting horn and the baying of hounds in my ears.

My grandfather developed a heart condition when I was about seven years of age and this made it impossible for him to walk very much. Polly and the jingle, a small, covered trap, were his means of transport from that time, and whenever possible I would go with him. He frequently had a heart attack while travelling, when he would have to take a tablet and was glad of my help at that time. It was during these journeys along the lanes of Hartland that I learnt so many things from my grandfather about life in general, but more especially about farming matters. He would point out various methods of practice by different farmers as we jogged along behind Polly. When we came to a hill, if grandfather was with us, my brother and I would get out of the jingle and walk. Polly had learnt a few tricks about pulling the jingle up a hill. Instead of going straight up in the middle of the road, she went up diagonally, from one side of the road to the other because she had discovered it was easier that way. I think poor Polly would be in dire trouble today with all the traffic, if she tried that method. The only vehicle one would be likely to meet in those days was another horse and carriage. Polly lived to the remarkable age of forty-two before I had to have her put down, and it was as though we had lost a relative when she was no longer with us.

Another favourite pet was an owl whom we called Barny. He was rescued by my brother and me after his mother had died. When Barny became a mature bird we released him into the open, but he never lost contact with us. Often when I was walking through our farmyard late at night, Barny would suddenly appear out of the darkness and perch on my shoulder. Or, in response to a special whistle which he had learnt to recognise, there would be an answering call from among the tall elm trees, and almost immediately two ghostly eyes would be looking into mine as if to say, 'I'm still here'. But one winter's night, when I arrived home late, there was no response to my whistle, and another pal had passed out of my life.

One of the great joys that was mine as a small boy was collecting eggs. In those days our hens roamed free and could go where they pleased; this meant that they laid their eggs in all kinds of out-of-the-way places and my job was to find their nests and collect the eggs. I searched hedges and climbed on to the straw ricks and into the lofts of the cattle sheds. Sometimes I discovered a nest with as many as twenty eggs, but I always left one because if the hen returned to lay again and found the nest empty, she would promptly desert that nest and make another elsewhere. Occasionally a nest would not be discovered and after three weeks or so a hen would be seen proudly strolling through the yard with her brood of a dozen or more chicks.

The poultry side of the farming business

was always left to the ladies of the household. They not only looked after the egg production department, but also reared chickens for their own table and for sale. Many also reared turkeys, geese and ducks for the Christmas market. I well remember all the trouble that used to be taken in rearing turkeys, especially. They seemed ready to get every disease imaginable and to be ready to die at almost any moment; they were very difficult to rear. As children we were sent out to collect goose grass, known to us as 'clider'; this was chopped very finely and mixed with the young turkeys' food, and was supposed to aid their delicate digestive systems. During the fattening period, some two months before Christmas, the turkeys were 'crammed'; this meant that the food had to be physically pushed down each turkey's throat every day until their crops were completely full; otherwise they would not eat enough to get them fat for the festive season.

It was always hoped that the weather would be cold for some ten to fourteen days before Christmas, because the poultry was killed and dressed during that time and would keep in better condition in cold weather — there being no refrigerators or other cooling systems at that time. The normal life of the farm would be completely disrupted during those days as one of the men would have to do the actual killing while the ladies picked off the feathers and dressed the birds. This was usually done in the kitchen in front of the open fire, with the bird held on the lap. A very useful garment used by the ladies for this work, and in fact for many other jobs around the farmhouse and outside, was the 'touser'. This was an apron made out of a hessian bag which had been cut open, and tape sewn at the top. On most farms the womenfolk fed the calves and the pigs, so they needed such strong protective clothing. After the poultry had been picked, the best of the feathers, especially those from the ducks and geese, were retained and used for pillows and mattresses after they had been baked in the oven to sterilise them.

I kept ferrets, too, but they were more than just pets; they were bred to drive rabbits out of their burrows so that we could shoot them or catch them in nets, as we did before we were old enough to have gun licences. The nets were placed over the rabbit holes in such a way that when the ferret drove the rabbit out, it became tangled in the net and we were able to catch it. At a very early age we learnt to give its neck a little twist and it would be dead instantly. In those days rabbits were so numerous as to be a scourge to farmers. Not only did they eat a great deal of grass and corn, but because of the smell they left behind, no stock would graze after them.

The great rabbiting day of the year was Boxing Day. On that day a very early start would be made to feed and water the stock before setting off with the ferrets and guns, to spend all the day driving out rabbits. When darkness fell, we would troop in with our 'bag' — anything up to fifty or sixty rabbits. The ferrets then had to be fed and all the daily chores of milking and feeding the cattle carried out. After this we sat down to a wonderful meal with many friends and relatives. The rest of the evening, often until 2 am, would be spent in singing, dancing and games.

Another day to which we looked forward was Old Christmas Day as we called it. This was January 6th — a very popular day for parties of all kinds. If a party was held too far from home to walk, we were taken by horse and cart, and later by pony and jingle. We nearly always went to Hartland Quay on that day, where an aunt and uncle kept a small hotel at the bottom of a steep winding road, ending almost at the water's edge. Here again, we had great fun, but often we had to start for home in the teeth of a howling gale which was strong enough to hold one's weight as one leaned against it. Polly would struggle up that hill carrying the ladies, while the men and boys walked, often having to help Polly by pushing on the jingle. The only lights we had were two carriage lamps lit by candles which flickered all the way home. Sometimes we did not reach home until two or three o'clock in the morning, but there was always such a sense of satisfaction after these occasions which seems to be lacking today. Perhaps it was because we had to make our own fun as there was no radio let alone television and transistors in those days.

A rather nice custom that we observed on the eve of Old Christmas Day, was giving the stock an extra meal. Late in the evening, as we made our final inspection of the stock before going to bed, we carried around a special treat for each of the animals. In the shippons the cows would be lying comfortably on their beds, contentedly chewing the cud in an atmosphere of peace. In the fatstock sheds, too, there would be grunts and puffs as those sweating beasts put on more and more weight. The horses always seemed to be chewing day and night; but on that night, one found them quietly resting on their bedding or standing asleep on their feet. This is how we found the stock every night, but Old Christmas Eve was different. Armed with some choice cattle cake, I could barely get inside the doors of the sheds before the animals were on their feet, sniffing the air in expectation. Within a few minutes thay had licked their troughs clean and, as if to say thank you, gave me a final lick of the hand with their rough tongues.

All this may seem to some to be sloppy and sentimental, but there was, at least for me a very real meaning behind it. Many of those animals, especially the horses and cows, had been reared on the farm and were part of the family, so it seemed quite natural to share with them some of our celebrations. But most of all for me, it was a little act of thanksgiving for the privilege of sharing the life of the animals closely day by day; something which perhaps only one who has been born and brought up among farm animals can fully appreciate. An old story says that the animals fall on their knees in adoration at midnight on the eve of Old Christmas Day. Well, I have been with them on many occasions at that hour, but the only time I have seen them go on their knees is when they lie down or get up!

My schooldays at Hartland went swiftly by. We had the usual childish illnesses, and there were times when there was illness in the family, but I cannot remember ever being unhappy. In some wonderful way, any unhappy days of childhood have been obliterated, while the happy days stand out clear and fresh.

Some months before my fourteenth birthday, my parents decided that it would be good for me to spend a year or two away from home, at a school where I could improve my education generally, but mainly so that I could learn to stand on my own feet, as they put it. So just one month after my birthday I was put on a train at Bideford with a ticket to Colchester in Essex, via Waterloo and Liverpool Street stations in London. I had never been on a train, let alone been to London. It is not easy for anyone nowadays, when travelling by train, car and air is so commonplace — even for young people — to realise what a trauma it was for a lad of my age, who had never been further than twenty miles from home, to be suddenly thrust out into the unknown.

Crossing London was a nightmare experience; I had never dreamt there could be a place of such confusion and uproar, but I felt more at home on reaching Colchester, because my mother's parents lived there and I was to stay with them. The Technical College I attended there specialised in practical skills, such as engineering and carpentry, but also had an emphasis on related subjects such as geometry and maths. I was glad to find that I could keep up with the boys of Essex and that my little school back in Devon had not let me down.

Educationally, I settled easily, but what proved to be almost impossible for a long time was understanding the Essex dialect. They, in their turn, had great difficulty in trying to decipher mine — it must have been to them almost a foreign language. In fact I doubt if they ever really understood all I said.

My first letter home expressed my disgust and unhappiness; but slowly I came to enjoy life there. It opened new horizons for me and I began to realise that there was a wide world beyond my little sphere of life in a tiny corner of Devon, which offered tremendous possibilites for me. It is difficult for anyone these days to understand how limited a fourteen-year-old's knowledge of life could be at that time, in such an isolated part of the country. There were no newspapers, unless fetched from a long distance, whilst radio and television, as I have said, were unknown. So little did we know of the outside world that I heard men saying when they came home after the 1914–18 war, that at the time they were called up, they did not know what it was all about.

During my time at Colchester, the General Strike of 1926 took place. My maternal grandfather, with whom I stayed while at school, was an Inspector on what was then the London and North Eastern Railway out of Liverpool Street Station. He was a non-union man, so when the trains came to a halt, I used to go with him each morning and evening to the railway station to feed and water cattle that had been left in their trucks in the sidings. We had to pass through the picket lines in order to do this, but not once was my grandfather challenged on what those pickets knew to be an errand of mercy.

Towards the end of my first year in Essex, disaster struck our farm back in Devon. On July 19th a strip of land half a mile wide across the peninsula of Hartland was devastated by a terrible storm. All the crops were destroyed and the livestock had to be sold before winter, as there was nothing on which to feed them. Because of this my parents were unable to meet the cost of keeping me at school, and at Christmas 1926 I returned to my old home and to the old way of life; but now it was with a new vision of what it was all about. The influence of the school in Colchester, and especially of my mother's parents who were wonderful people, laid a solid foundation for my future though I did not become aware of it until many years had passed.

Looking back at that time, it is surprising that on coming home from Essex I did not branch out into an entirely different job of work, but two things influenced me in my decision to pick up the farming threads again. The first was my deep-rooted love of the land and of farm stock. Secondly, it was expected of the elder son that he would continue the family tradition; but I really did not need the latter influence in making my choice.

7

Working with Cattle and Making Music

So it was on that cold January morning in 1927 that I struggled out of bed to begin a new life. We wore thick cord breeches for work in the winter, with a pair of heavy hob-nailed boots and leather leggings; and a pair of more refined breeches, polished boots and leggings for market days. If it rained when we worked out of doors, we wore a thick hessian sack across our shoulders, like a cape, and another round our waist in the form of an apron. These kept us warm as well as dry and were easily exchanged for others when they became soaked with rain. Wellington boots, which most farmers now wear in wet weather, were unknown at that time. No one went without a hat in those days; a cap was usually worn because it was not so easily blown off by the wind.

Work on the farms at that time was divided into three main categories. There was the 'horseman' who did all the ploughing and tilling and other jobs where horses were involved; the 'bullock' man who did the milking and fed and tended to the livestock; and there was what was known as the 'stand-to-work man' who undertook many skilled manual jobs. On our farm my cousin Tom was the horseman, Jim Peard was the stand-to-work man, and my father looked after the stock.

I was delegated to work with my father for the first two years. Milking the cows was always the first job to be done each morning, and again in the evening, seven days a week; then the stock of varying ages were fed and watered if it was winter time and they were lying in the sheds. Shippons had to be cleaned out every day and fresh bedding put down for all the stock. Hay was cut out of the ricks in three foot squares, using a knife shaped like a guillotine with a handle across the top, and it was then carried to all the sheds where the cattle were housed. Mangolds and turnips had to be sliced into pieces through a machine which was turned by hand, then mixed with chaff before being fed to the cattle. The calves were fed with milk twice daily — as I had done when a small boy.

During the winter months when the cattle were 'laying in', the corn had to be ground into meal. This was usually done in the evenings, when a small petrol engine drove a mill through which the corn passed between two metal plates. This same engine also worked a chaff-cutter and straw was cut for the horses and other stock. Before these little engines became available, horses were used for this work. In a shed known as a 'round house', a horse was harnessed to a horizontal metal wheel some twelve feet in diameter which was pivoted on a post in the centre of the shed. This wheel had cogs on its upper side which connected with a small cog wheel fastened to the wall, the latter joined to a shaft with pulleys. These in turn drove the mill and chaff-cutter when the horse went round and round the shed, rotating the big wheel. This was an efficient and cheap way of working barn machinery. Some horses did not even need to be led, but went on alone. The difficulty arose when the horse suddenly decided to take a rest or to knock off a fly — then everything stopped.

Another important job for the stockman was the preparation of the cattle for market. Most of the calves we reared were intended for beef, which meant they were encouraged to grow quickly and become as heavy as possible in the shortest period of time. The public demand in those days was for what was known as 'baby beef' — that is, animals under the age of two years, and weighing around ten hundredweight. This applied to lambs as well: these were bred for the Easter market, which meant that they had to be born early in January when the weather was not always conducive to easy working.

With sheep and cows there were quite often difficult births. These we had to deal with ourselves, except in the more severe cases when a veterinary surgeon would be called in. He lived fourteen miles away, so we had to learn to cope with problems ourselves whenever possible. I had seen hundreds of births while growing up; to me it was just a normal part of life to help in difficult cases. So when the time came for me to operate alone, it was all so natural. In most cases no human help was needed, but in some multiple births there was the danger that one or more of the offspring might wander away and get cold; in this way they might die before they had found their mother's milk. This was especially so in the cold of winter; then it was that the open fire in the kitchen proved to be so valuable, along with a drop of brandy, in restoring the tiny creatures to life. I often used to take a chair into the shed where a sow was farrowing and sit there several hours during the night to make sure that all was well during her labour.

But everything did not always go right with

the livestock. There were times of sickness and disease; at that time there were no preventative serums for contagious abortion, for instance, and during one particular year every calf born was premature and dead. This meant not only the loss of the calf, but the milk from the cows was severely diminished also. This abortion rapidly spread from farm to farm over a wide area and was a great great blow to the finances of the farming community. This sometimes happened in a flock of sheep: many lambs would be born prematurely, and this, along with twin-lamb disease, which was also quite common at that time, caused a substantial reduction in our income. Accidents, too, were a source of much concern. I remember how one of our younger horses had to be put down after having been pushed into a hedge by other horses and had become impaled on the stump of a small tree. Another very promising two-year-old was bitten by a snake and subsequently died.

A monthly livestock market was started in January 1914 in a field adjoining the village. The auctioneers, Messrs Kivell and Sons from Holsworthy, held such markets in many villages in that area. There was no transport to take stock to a big central market as is done today: cattle and sheep had to walk up to four miles to the small markets dotted about the countryside, while pigs were taken there by horse and butt. Dealers and butchers from a wide area attended these sales, as well as farmers from the better grazing lands of Somerset and other counties, to buy store cattle to turn into beef. All our pigs were sold as 'weaners' — that is, at eight to ten weeks of age — and realised twenty five to thirty shillings each. A two-year-old fat bullock would be sold for about fifteen to twenty pounds, while a freshly calved cow — what we called a renewed cow — and her calf would fetch twenty to thirty pounds. Fat lambs in those days averaged around two pounds each, while a breeding ewe would sell for five pounds.

There were no pens for the cattle at the market: each farmer's stock had to be kept in a bunch beside the hedge, all around the field. Sometimes we had to stand there for anything up to four hours, often in wet weather, before our turn came to put the cattle through the sale ring. After they had been sold, they were taken home again and kept until the buyer was ready for them. This was often as long as three weeks; and then they had to be walked as much as eight miles to a common rendezvous with other farmers' stock, to meet the buyer's drovers who then took the whole lot a similar distance to the buyer's farm or to the railway station. This meant that we often had to leave home long before it was daylight in the winter. Our journey took us over an open moor where the cattle sometimes escaped off the road and had to be chased across boggy land in the dark.

It is said that a stockman is born and not made, and I believe this is true. There seems to be an inbuilt ability to look after all kinds of stock: either you can anticipate the reaction of a particular animal or you can't and that makes all the difference between success and failure as a stockman. In the winter time, particularly, I had to spend many hours of each day with the animals. From seven o'clock in the morning my days were devoted to feeding and cleaning, and caring for the sick animals. Even when I went out in the evening, the cattle had to be 'tended up' as we called it on returning home, no matter how late it was. This meant that the cows and fattening bullocks were given their last feed for the night, and at the same time we inspected them to make sure that none were 'blown' or 'bloated' — a form of indigestion which causes the body to swell and which could end in death.

But life for me was not all hard work, even

though I enjoyed it immensely. When I was about ten years old, my mother insisted that I learn to play the piano. I was taught at first by Miss Olive Taylor, whose father kept a draper's shop in the village: later I was taught by Auriely Clay, the daughter of a lighthouse keeper at Hartland Point. Auriely used to cycle the four miles to our farm every Saturday, up and down those steep hills in all kinds of weather, to give me lessons. I was, and still am, so grateful for what she did for me because music was to become in later years a most wonderful hobby. I owe such a lot to my mother, also, who used to lock me in the room with the piano until I had done half an hour's practice each evening. Two years later I started to take lessons on the violin with Frank Christmas, the local postmaster. Frank was an accomplished musician whose talents were never fully utilised. I owe so much to him — not only as a teacher, but as a friend.

When I was seventeen the Hartland Parochial Church Council asked me and two friends, Charlie Barter and George Burrow, if we would like to have lessons on the organ. Mr Mills had been the organist at the parish church for many years and was getting rather frail, so the council offered to pay the cost of our training with the hope that we might be ready to take over his job when he decided to retire. We had some two years of lessons from a brilliant organist at Northam, then Mr Mills died and we began to play for the services in the church on a rota basis, which I enjoyed very much.

During the year after I left school I decided, along with four friends, to form a dance band. Dancing was a very popular pastime then, but the organisers always had to hire a band from a long distance, or make do with a second-rate piano. So we formed the Silver Star Orchestra: Charlie Barter on the piano, Sid Williams on violin, Tom Squance on trumpet and banjo, Des Wood on the drums, and myself on saxophone and clarinet — two instruments I had been quietly practising for some time. We modelled ourselves on the dance bands of the time whose playing we listened to with great interest — Jack Payne, The Savoy Orpheans and the like.

We had a beautiful motif painted on the bass drum in the fashion of the time by Percy Beer, a talented artist who had been a school pal. The band proved to be a great success and remained so for ten years, with only one change in personnel: Des Wood was replaced by Bill Squance. We practised one evening a week at the home of the pianist's parents and

I have marvelled since at the tolerance and understanding shown by Mr and Mrs Barter in allowing us to come in to their home and make what must have been for them something of a noise. They were getting rather old at that time, but still they made us very welcome and there was always a cup of tea when we finished playing.

We played at dances an average of two or three nights each week during the winter months, covering North Devon and North Cornwall. We were also engaged to play at dinner dances at some of the 'big houses' as they were called; in those days it was normally the home of the 'squire' of a village, and in these homes we were treated right royally. All this gave us great satisfaction and joy, even though we used to play from eight in the evening until one o'clock the next morning for the princely sum of five shillings plus our travelling expenses. It was a wonderful way of meeting people from outside our immediate neighbourhood, and for one or two of us it was the way we met our future partners in life — but more about that later.

I also became interested at that time in the local village band — the Hartland Town Band, as it was called. The bass drummer resigned and I took his place briefly before going to play the clarinet. There were twenty-six of us in that band and we played at various outdoor functions such as the Garden Show and on Remembrance Sunday, as well as at other sporting events in the village and outside. We played at many village carnivals in North Devon, where we were joined by other bands from surrounding villages. We practised on Tuesday evenings, so that almost every evening of my week was occupied with music of one kind or another. On reflection, the quality of our playing was not very high in either band, but that was secondary to the fact that we enjoyed ourselves immensely, and at the same time provided a service for the community, the majority of whom thought our playing was superb. This is easy to understand when one remembers that it was the first time they had heard or seen a dance band in action. It must have seemed a great improvement on the out-of-tune piano or the wheezy accordian which had been their only means of accompaniment for as long as they could remember. I feel so grateful to all those lads of both bands who gave me such joy by their comradeship, and of whom at the time of writing only Sid Williams and myself remain of the original dance band, and myself alone of the Town Band.

Other hobbies of which I was very fond

were what we called the Health and Strength Club and the Boxing Club. In the former we did weightlifting and gymnastics and the training that went with these activities. Both these clubs were held in the barn at Norton, the home of Tom Squance who was a member of the two bands with me. On looking back I wonder how we found the time to fit all our activities into our short leisure time.

8

My Pals the Horses

At the end of two years as bullock man, I was promoted to horseman. Of all the jobs on the farm, I enjoyed working with horses most of all. A wonderful comradeship is built up between a man and his team; the horses sometimes seem to be almost human in their response and they get to know one's every whim. A horseman spent long hours alone with his team — both in the fields and in the stable in the evenings — and I used to talk to mine as if they were human. They would often turn their heads and look at me when I spoke and the expression in their eyes made me almost expect them to speak.

From the time I was a very small boy, when out in the fields with Tom while he was ploughing, I had been allowed to hold the plough and had learnt how to handle the reins, so it was only a matter of becoming strong enough to manage the plough in order to take over the job completely.

My team was called Jessie and Blossom. They were shires, and when I took them over they were nine and ten years old respectively. Blossom was the most sweet tempered mare it was possible to find: I never once knew her to become ruffled or disturbed. No matter what she was asked to do, whether it was in the shafts drawing hay or corn, or in chains ploughing, cultivating or tilling, you could depend on Blossom to do her job without a fuss. Jessie was of a rather different temperament. She did her work well, but little things seemed to disturb her at times. A sharp word from me early in the morning would upset her and she would not forget it the whole day. She had a little habit of throwing her head in the air when she thought I was angry with her and she would turn her head round at me as if to say, 'You've started on me again.'

Both these mares had been reared on our farm, so I knew them from birth. I had seen them grow into two-year-old fillies and then be 'broken in'. Charlie Turner did this, who was an expert at training horses for shaft work and chains. They then settled down to the routine of farm work, working alongside an old horse we called Farmer until they became familiar with their tasks. They became so well trained that they needed very little rein to guide them: a word for each manoeuvre was sufficient. If I wished them to turn to the left, the word was 'cummeer'; if a right turn was required, the command was 'wug off', and to stop, it was 'wow'. I don't know where these words came from except perhaps the first. A horse was always led on its left side, so when the leader wished it to come to the left — towards him — he would naturally say, 'Come here'. It always amazed me how straight a team of horses could walk hour after hour.

Ploughing was one of the jobs I enjoyed doing most. A day's work for a team of horses and a single furrow plough was always reckoned to be one acre. The swish of the ploughshare as it cut through the soil, especially when it was grassland that was being ploughed, and the pleasant sound of the furrow being packed into the right position are sounds that have been with me all my life. The rattle of the chains and the occasional snort from the horses, along with the screaming and squawking of the seagulls were sounds which contributed to a wonderfully pleasant job. Only a few minutes after starting to plough in the morning there would be a screaming host of gulls of several species swooping and diving into the furrow just ploughed only a yard or so behind one's feet; they gobbled up worms and other grubs and fought and squabbled. Day after day one would recognise the same birds — the youngsters of the previous summer pushing their way into the fray, with the stately old cock birds trying to keep some sort of order. There would be the bird with only one leg — the other probably having been smashed against a rock during a gale — they would all be there, day after day.

There was always a very keen but friendly rivalry between neighbouring ploughmen, not only in producing good work, but also in the way the horses and their harness was 'turned out'. Good workmanship in ploughing not only looks good, but makes all the difference to the ease and efficiency of cultivating in the spring. If the furrow had been thrown over too flat, it took much longer to produce a 'tilth' than if it had been set up on edge. The art of ploughing a straight and even furrow came with much practice by both man and horses. This was especially so when 'cutting in', that is, ploughing the first thin furrow across the middle of the field towards a point on the hedge on the far side. One slight deviation by the horses, or a glance behind by the ploughman, could lead to such a twist in the furrow that it would be almost impossible to put it right. Having made the mistake there was no going back and starting again.

I found great joy in the stable, too. The day

began at seven o'clock when I watered the horses and fed them with oats and hay, then the stable was cleaned out before going into the house for my own breakfast. By eight o'clock the horses were harnessed and ready to start work in the field. At half past ten I stopped for lunch, usually a cup of tea and bread and cheese or a piece of saffron cake. This was taken sitting in the hedge, while the horses nibbled the grass. At one o'clock the horses were taken into the stable for water and a feed of oats and chaff, while I had my dinner. Two o'clock saw us on our way back to the field where we would work until five or half past in the summer.

After tea, when the horses had cooled down, they had to be groomed and prepared for the night. The harness, too, was cleaned and the brasses polished. I knew of no more pleasant place to be on cold or wet winter evenings than in a stable. The unique smell of horses and sweet hay, combined with rhythmic chewing of oats and hay and the fellowship and conversation of like-minded friends, in the warmth created by the bodies of the horses as we relaxed on a bundle of straw after a hard day in the fields, was really wonderful — a memory that will remain with me until my dying day.

Late in the evening, sometimes in the early

hours of the morning after returning from a dance, I would look in at the horses to make sure that all was well and that there was no sign of colic or other problems which sometimes arose when horses which had been doing heavy work were confined to the stable.

During frosty weather when the ground was too hard to plough, there was always plenty for the horses to do. Dung had to be got out into the fields. This was placed in small heaps about nine paces apart in rows up and down the field, and was later spread by Jim Peard. Wood had to be brought into the yard to be sawn up for the open fire, and in the event of a long spell of frosty weather, when all the horse work had been completed, the horses still needed to be exercised each day.

As the days grew longer and the spring arrived, life for the horseman grew more hectic. There was artificial fertiliser to be spread on the grass fields and as soon as the ploughed fields dried out sufficiently, the 'breaking down' began — the harrowing, rolling and drilling of the corn. Each of these was a joy in itself: to see that lovely straight furrow over which one had taken such care and pride just crumbling into lovely 'tilth', and the corn being drilled into a beautiful, moist, warm seedbed, was something that gave pleasure to every horseman.

Towards the end of April, according to the weather at the time, the horses were put out to grass at night. I'm not quite sure who looked forward to this event most, the horses or the horseman. The sense of relief the horses expressed as they rolled and galloped in their new-found freedom, after nearly six months of being confined to the stable, was something that had to be seen to be believed. For me it meant that there was no stable to be cleaned out each day and no hay to be carried from the rick to the stable — all of which made a nice break, even though I enjoyed all the work so much.

During early May the fields where hay would eventually be cut had to be chain-harrowed and rolled after the stones had been picked. At this time, too, mangolds had to be tilled, and then the swedes and other turnips. Then came the hay harvest in June, which was perhaps the hardest and hottest work the horses were asked to do. The heavy pole which carried the mowing machine was strapped to the horses' neck-collar, and pulled from the same collar by chains. The horses were subjected to a great deal of stress, especially when the grass was difficult to cut and the machine had to be constantly reversed. I remember how relieved they seemed to be at the end of a day of grass cutting, and they were let out into their field for the night. They would immediately roll and roll on the ground, as if savouring the cool grass on their overheated bodies, before shaking themselves and settling down to munch their way through the quiet hours of the night.

Hay harvest seems to have been a much more exciting time in those days than it is today. The work was much harder, of course, but because there were always many more men engaged in the work, it always seemed to be done in a lighthearted way. As an example of the pleasure we experienced at that time, when we were carrying hay into ricks we always had two or three spare picks beside the gate of the hay field, and almost always some friend from the village, or a neighbour whose hay was not ready on that particular day, would come at some time during the evening to lend a helping hand. There was no question of paying so much an hour — this was unheard of — because in the case of the neighbour we should be doing the same for him within a day or so. The friend from the village was quite satisfied with his fill of cider from the stone jar kept in the shade of the hedge, and with the wonderful supper which was always provided when the day's work was finished.

An interesting operation in hay harvesting, unique to that time, was 'poking'. The hay would have been turned over two or three times, but always there would be a little that lay tight on the ground and would not have dried sufficiently. So by poking, that is, putting the hay into small heaps, all was cleared from the ground. Also it was done to keep the majority of hay dry if it was likely to rain before the next day. This was usually done during the evening, often working until it became dark. When we were young it seemed to us rather a waste of time, because by eleven o'clock the next morning the pokes would all have to be spread about again to dry in the sun and wind. This was even more frustrating when we had planned to go somewhere in the evening.

As horseman, it was part of my job to bring in the hay and corn with one of my team and a wagon or cart. In doing this I had to learn how to make a load secure enough that it did not fall over on the way to the ricks. There were no rubber-tyred wheels on the carts in those days, so the loads were subjected to a lot of bumping on the rough tracks from the fields. Sometimes a second horse was needed to help pull the load up a steep hill. The job of leading it was usually a boy's job and one which my brother and I did before leaving school.

When the corn was nearly ripe there was a great deal of activity in preparation for the harvest ahead. We used a reaper in my young days to cut the corn. This was done by a man riding on the machine with a kind of wide rake with which he 'taithed' the corn into bundles. He did this by allowing the cut corn to collect on a kind of platform until there was sufficient for a sheaf. This was then tipped off with the rake; other men would follow and bind the sheaves with a few strands of the same straw.

All this was changed with the introduction of the self-binder. This machine was undoubtedly the forerunner of mechanisation on the farms, and from that time many old methods which had been in use for a great many years gradually gave way to new ideas. I well remember the first time we prepared to use our new self-binder. It took almost the whole of one day to put the canvases, which carried the corn to where it was to be tied into sheaves, in their correct places. We also had to learn how to dismantle the machine so that it could be taken along a road to another field and reassembled to start cutting the corn there. Many was the heated argument between my father and grandfather; the latter could not see much use for ‘these new-fangled contraptions’, as he put it. But when he saw it working he, too, marvelled at the wonderful way it cut the corn and tied it into neat sheaves, with all the saving of back-breaking labour.

There was always a lighter side to cutting the corn, whether it was by reaper or self-binder, and that was trying to catch the rabbits that congregated in the corn. As children we chased them with one of the dogs as they came out into the open. The machine would go round and round, with the area of standing corn getting smaller and smaller, and the rabbits finding a decreasing space in which to hide. At last, one, then another, would make a dash for the safety of a distant hedge with the children and dogs in hot pursuit, zig-zagging over and around the sheaves and often falling over them. Only occasionally did we catch a rabbit. Sometimes we had a surprise, and instead of rabbits bolting out of the corn a fox would suddenly go careering across the field; but there was never any hope of catching that wily fellow. Foxes often did considerable damage to a field of corn by rolling in it and flattening it so much that it could not be cut.

As soon as the corn was cut the sheaves were stood up into ‘shocks’, or stooks as some people called them. There it remained for anything up to a fortnight in the case of oats, which was always cut while it was still a little green. Wheat, on the other hand, was cut in a much riper state and stayed in the field for only a day or two if the weather was good. But I can remember years when the weather was anything but kind; in fact there were times when we did not get enough consecutive dry days to get all the corn in a fit condition to carry it into the ricks. I have seen corn in the fields in the middle of December, by which time the sheaves had grown green with the sprouting corn. But the weather was not always bad and the last load of corn to be brought in was the signal for great rejoicing. That evening there would be an extra good supper with plenty of beer and cider.

The end of the corn harvest did not mean that the horseman and his team could take a break. We immediately began to prepare for the next year's crop. The first job was to clean the ground where the previous crop had grown. This was done by what we called 'skirting', a very shallow form of ploughing — just deep enough to get under the roots of the weeds. After a few days of dry weather, the ground was harrowed and the weed rolled up by the chain-harrows, after which we set about what was known as 'burning beat' —

putting the dried weed into heaps and setting it alight. I have memories of a lovely aroma drifting across the fields in the warm, golden days of autumn. The field was then left for a few weeks, for any remaining weeds to germinate, after which it was ploughed in the usual way, starting the horseman's year all over again.

In between his main work the horseman would see that the horses were kept well shod. This was a job for Stan Dayman, who was a craftsman at this work. How he held up the feet and legs of those great shires day after day, enveloped in the smoke of burning hooves as he pared and trimmed them to make a good fit for the shoes, was a mystery to me. He used to say that it was his daily ration of 'New Inn beer' that kept him going.

Finally, there was the day that the horses came in from the fields in the autumn to prepare for their winter work; then they were clipped. This was Charlie Turner's job, which he did with great skill even though the horses were sometimes very ticklish and objected violently to his clippers; so much in fact, that some had only to hear the whirr of the machine to become upset.

9

Other Work on the Farm

After I had worked with the horses for two years, my brother took them over and I went on to do 'stand-to-work' jobs. These included rick making, thatching, hedging, hoeing roots, shearing sheep and many other jobs as the season came around. Then there was the veterinary work, such as castrating calves, lambs and pigs and knowing the right use of drugs for particular complaints. There was also the business side of the farm: the accounts, as well as the buying and selling of livestock, produce, seeds and manures.

Hedging was a very important art to be learnt — not only because good hedges meant livestock could be kept securely in the fields, but also because all the farm tenancy agreements stated that any hedge that was not in good repair would be chargeable to the outgoing tenant and this could involve a considerable sum of money. The success of hedging lay in making sure that each 'clat' or turf was placed in such a position as to let the rain into each row below, as the hedge was built, otherwise it would become dry and die. When the bank was complete, the bushes on the top were 'steeped' — that is, they were partly cut through with an axe, and laid flat on the top. When spring came they sprouted and made a good thick hedge. This work went on from November to March, except during frosty weather.

Hoeing was a back-breaking job which took place during several weeks in May and June. Three or four acres had to be hoed several times: first to thin out the roots, and then at intervals to kill the weeds. We were always glad when the crop was hoed for the last time. During the intervals between hoeing, another equally tiring job had to be done. This was sheep shearing, which was done towards the middle of June if the weather was right. The breed of sheep we kept were Devon Longwools; they were big and heavy and had to be held upright while being sheared. We used hand shears in those days and these had to be kept in good cutting condition; this was an art in itself. Shearing was very hot work because it was usually done in the barn and the combination of the heat of the sheep's body and the grease which came out of the wool caused us to perspire — so much so, that the sweat dropped on to the wool as we worked.

Of all the jobs I did in this category of farm work, the most interesting, and that which needed the greatest expertise, was the making and thatching of hay and corn ricks. For corn, especially, great care had to be taken to ensure that the sheaves were placed in such a position that the rain would run off. This meant that the middle of the rick had to be kept full and a little higher than the outside. The rick was then ready for thatching. Wheat straw, which had been specially prepared, was used for this. Instead of the sheaves of wheat being put through the threshing machine in the ordinary way, only the ears of the wheat were threshed out, leaving the straw straight and stiff rather than broken up, as would be the case if it had been threshed. This method was called 'combing', and the resulting 'reed' as it was called was, and still is, used to thatch houses as well as ricks.

Two men usually thatched together, starting at one end of the rick with one on either side. They placed the reed in layers — 'lain upon lain' as it was called, in three foot widths, starting from the eaves, or 'auvis' and going up to the 'ridge' or top of the rick. This was securely tied down with thick hessian cords spaced nine inches apart along the length of the rick. Because of the severe gales that swept in from the Atlantic, further cords had to be placed over the top of the rick, at right angles to the others, and some three feet apart; on these were tied heavy pebbles from the beach. The job was completed by trimming and tidying the rick; what a lovely sight those rows of corn ricks made, all safely thatched before the winter rains.

There were many other jobs that a stand-to-work had to do in the course of a year. The last one in the farming year was pulling mangolds. This was usually done in early October, or once the roots were ripe. Two rows at a time were pulled and the tops cut off; the roots were then placed in such a way that four rows were piled into one for the horseman to put into a butt. Many a finger was sliced in doing this work, as the knife was used in a quick upward movement, close to the hand. The mangolds were brought into the yard and placed in 'camps' or heaps, covered first with straw and then with earth and bracken to keep out the frost, mangolds being very susceptible to this form of damage. They were eaten by the cattle and sheep in late winter and early spring.

Swimming was a very popular pastime for many of us during the summer months. Many a time, after a long hot day in the hay or corn field, we got on our bikes and dashed down to one of the little coves — usually

Speke's Mill because it was the nearest — and plunged into the cool waters of the great ocean. Quite often it was dark before we left home so that we swam by moonlight. After a rest we clambered up the zig-zagging cliff path, and home to fall into bed to sleep, with the blissful assurance of another wonderful day tomorrow.

Speke's Mill was the scene of much activity in the days when I was growing up. Harry Balsdon supplied builders and farmers with sand from the beach. He used six donkeys with panniers to get it to the top of the cliff from where it could be collected. Each donkey was loaded up with about two hundredweight of sand; it then staggered across the rocks and pools, up the steep, two-hundred-foot cliff path alone, and waited patiently beside a huge heap of sand until Harry came up with the last donkey; they were then unloaded. This process would then start all over again until the incoming tide stopped the work. After work the donkeys were put in a field at the cliff top until the tide was right to start the work the next day.

We had some wonderful neighbours during my teenage years, some of whom had been pals of my school days. One's neighbours in a farming community are very important people. Farmers depend a great deal upon one another for help in all kinds of situations; loaning each other implements and in many other ways. It was also true in a social sense, for in my young days there was little or no transport and we lived so far from the centres of population. Each family would know what was going on in the next home and any variation in the general routine of life would at once bring someone to see if all was well. I well remember once noticing a light shining in the kitchen of Leigh Farm, across the valley from my home, at three o'clock in the morning. We knew something must be wrong and on investigating we found that our dear neighbour, Mr William Pillman, had accidently stepped over the bank of a stream and had drowned. Occurrences such as that bring people closer together everywhere, but this was especially true when we were much more dependent upon one another.

10

Heart Searchings

So my teenage years slipped quickly by; every moment filled to the limit with positive action, and during those years two things happened which were to have a lasting influence on my future life. At the age of fifteen I received the Sacrament of Confirmation at the hands of the Right Reverend Lord William Cecil, the Diocesan Bishop, in my home church at Stoke, along with several of my contemporaries. For several months before that happened, I had had occasional thoughts about the reality of my church-going, and indeed, of my belief in particular. I could not get out of my mind the thought that because I happened to have been born into a Christian family and had accepted what they believed, this was necessarily right for me. The conventional type of Christianity in which I had been brought up no longer satisfied me; I craved for a more dynamic personal relationship in my spiritual life.

After some months of heart searching, I finally decided to put the Christian faith on

one side completely and look at
other religions had to offer. I
opportunity to study Buddhism,
Confucianism and anything else w
could satisfy my desire for spiritua
ment. This I did at every c
sometimes while having my lunch
hedge when working in the fields
blessing was, as I look back, th
became obsessed with it, but ra
seemed the normal thing to be
seemed to be a part of growing up
animals and crops I tended
matured; I assumed that everybo
same at some time in their lives.

In my study of the great relig
world, my mind was very much b
found a God who loved all pe
where, not just a small minority
themselves Christians. But even
great spiritual leaders of long ag
Confucius and Mohammed, in
tremendously, they still did not
with the dynamic spirituality fo
yearned, and to which I could c
life. They were all dead prophets, a
they had nothing to offer me e
examples. The strange thing is
Christian teaching, too, had seem
me nothing more than those prop

to offer. Oh, yes, I had learnt about the urrection and the Ascension, but some- ' I had failed to grasp the reality of the itual. I could not accept the fact that there ld be any reality other than that which I ld discern through the senses; I was 'ching for another dimension without wing it.

or seven years I continued to search, and lually there dawned on me the fact that whole of Creation is but a reflection of Universal Spirit of Life, and whatever , is, or will be, whether formed or nless, exists in that Spirit, the Eternal v, who is God. Then it was that so much he teaching of my young days came alive me. I realised that if God was in all things, n He was in me and in all those whose s touched mine. The tremendous fact hit like a bomb — if I responded to the wledge that I can be at one with Him ough Christ, then everything falls into e as I let go and God takes over my life. s wonderful assurance gave me great ce of mind and life became so very ting.

'he second event which influenced my nage years a great deal was when my her started to take paying guests into our ne during the summer months. It was

almost as if I was meeting and talking to people from another world, just as I had done when at school in Essex. Some of our guests came year after year and became firm friends, and every September my mother's family came for their holiday — something to which we looked forward with great joy.

By this time, there were many people coming to our area for their holidays. Some of them continued to come for several years — in some cases up to the time of their retirement, then they would decide to buy a house or have one built and retire to where they had spent so many holidays. This was the beginning of a new approach to life by many local people. The old order was changing: people began to realise, as I had done, that there was a wide and interesting world outside their home parish. One such family who came to live at an adjoining cottage to our farm had a son who was a little younger than me. Philip Leigh and I became great friends; he was later ordained a priest and we have kept in contact ever since that time.

Our holiday friends must have been very surprised at the primitive manner in which we lived in the early twenties. But all this was soon to change — by 1933 we had a nice bathroom and indoor sanitation. What a transformation that was in our lives: no more midnight journeys down the garden path; no more waiting until everyone was in bed before having a bath in front of the fire. This was especially welcome after a hot day in the harvest field or after a dirty job on the farm.

A favourite hobby of our teenage years was to scour the beaches after a violent storm in the winter months, to see if anything useful had been deposited. I remember walking along the beach at Hartland Quay with two or three friends after one such storm, when we came across what we took at first to be the body of a man. On looking a little more closely we discovered that it was Jack Jeffrey, known to us all as 'Stoke Policeman'. Jack was a very popular figure in the village; he was no more than five feet tall and quite stout, and he liked his pint of beer. It was a great relief to find that Jack was not dead, as we had at first thought, but only drunk. The reason for his condition was that he had gone down to the beach early that morning and had found a small keg washed up by the tide. He had carried the keg to a spot above high water mark, and being unable to resist the temptation to see what it contained, had opened it by making a small hole in the bung. Having discovered it contained brandy, Jack had obviously become very thirsty, fixed the keg on a rock and laid on his back beneath it, allowing the precious liquid to drip into his mouth. When we found him he was full to overflowing. His mouth was still open with the brandy dripping into it and out at the sides. It was surprising that he had not choked. We carried him up the steep cliff path to his home at Stoke, but getting so drunk did not lessen his desire for alcohol. Several years later Jack worked for me on the farm and he insisted on being paid every two weeks, so that he worked on a rota basis — two weeks on and one week off. During the latter he recovered after spending his two weeks' wages on drink. He was a great character with whom to work, having a wonderful sense of humour and a kindly attitude towards everyone. It was a real sadness to all who knew Jack when he was eventually killed by a car while lying drunk in the road.

At Christmas time, carol singing played a big part in our festivities. People really appreciated the singing in those days: apart from church services it would be the only time they would hear Christmas music. Some of the carols we sang must have been unique to Hartland; I have never heard them sung anywhere else. The carol party usually started at the Anchor Inn which was kept by the Beer family for many years. The members of the carol party would black their faces with burnt cork, though why this was done I never discovered. Accompanied by an accordian player, or sometimes by two or three mandolines, the party set out to tour the parish, covering a part of it that night and the remainder on another evening if they survived the first effort.

There was no transport, so a walk of anything up to twelve miles was quite common, before arriving home tired and weary at four or five o'clock in the morning. There were quite often casualties who fell by the wayside during the night, due to too many drinks and mince pies. It was not just a matter of our being handed a few shillings after singing two or three carols; at almost every home, even at two or three in the morning, people would get up to welcome us with hot mince pies and drinks. After singing we often had to collect our fallen comrades and take them home.

There were no midnight services in church as there are today. Our first Communion service on Christmas Day was at seven o'clock. I have very happy memories of walking through the woods to the little church of St John in the village, known as the chapel-of-ease. This was the name given to a church used by the parishioners who could not easily get to the parish church, for their 'ease and comfort' in worship. Here, under the flickering oil lamps, and to the accompaniment of a wheezy old organ, we sang the age-old carols and heard again the immortal words, 'The word became flesh and dwelt among us'.

Many interesting old characters lived in Hartland when I was young, some of whom gave us a great deal of fun, as well as telling the stories of their young days in the last century. One such was Sam Cann, a great churchman who could always be found in his pew every Sunday whatever the weather. He always said, 'Amen' at the end of each prayer in a very loud voice quite a while after everyone else, and it always seemed to me that the priest waited for him before beginning the next prayer.

He was an old man when I was about to leave school and as boys we loved to engage him in conversation. He was very fond of his pipe, so just as he was about to apply a match to the tobacco, we would ask him a question which we knew would interest him. He became so engrossed in answering us that he continued to hold the lighted match in his hand until it burnt his fingers and he would throw it away in disgust. He then lit another and another with the same result, while we kept plying our questions, and the pipe was not lighted. I have seen him use almost a whole box of matches during one conversation.

Another fascinating character of those days was called Thomas Cory Burrow. Along with his two sisters he kept a paper shop for many years. He had a long beard and used to say that he had never shaved in his life. When asked why, he replied that his mother once told him that Jesus never shaved, so she felt he should not do so either. He owned one of the first cars to come to Hartland — a Morgan two-seater. I was still at school at the time. He kept this car in a tiny garage near the school and from time to time he would ask three or four of us to help him get it up the steep gradient into his shed. Our job was to provide more weight on the back to prevent the wheels from spinning, but instead of doing that we lifted the back of the little car and so made things worse. The poor old man — he seemed old to us, but he could not have been more than fifty — used to get so frustrated, until one day he realised what we were doing and we lost our job as car pushers.

Cory Burrow is best remembered for his monthly newspaper, *The Hartland and West Country Chronicle*. He produced this sixteen-page paper as proprietor, editor, manager, compositor, printer and publisher almost single-handed from 1894 until 1940, with detailed news and comments, not only about Hartland, but also from Clovelly, Woolsery, Welcombe, Morwenstowe and other parishes in the district. No item of news passed his notice, down to the fact that the first swallow had been seen on a certain day, or that someone had picked a primrose in December.

For many years the paper contained contributions by Mr R. Pearce Chope, a local squire and historian, on the history of Hartland, all in great detail. He reported every wedding and funeral with a complete list of all people present, together with those who sent wreaths at funerals and the most minute details of the brides' dresses at weddings. All this, along with the texts by the preachers at the various churches and chapels each month, as well as a detailed list of what had taken place in Hartland twenty, fifty and one hundred years previously and much more cost the reader just one penny in old money. Cory, as he was affectionately known, was also a lay preacher in the Methodist church and he would travel many miles each Sunday to take services in outlying chapels.

One other interesting character that I came

to know well was Mr Henry Haynes. His special interest was the Hartland Town Band which he followed on every possible occasion. If we needed new music or another instrument, Henry Haynes came forward with the money. He even sported a special uniform, similar to ours, but with extra refinements; he would take his place at the head of the band when we were on the march, his moustache especially waxed for the occasion. We knew him as 'Squire Haynes', he being one of three or four gentlemen of independent means who lived in the parish at that time, and who were an asset to various organisations by their generous financial support.

When I was sixteen my grandfather, with whom I had always lived, died at the age of sixty-seven and this event made a profound impression on my life. It was the first time I had encountered a death in the family. I had seen my father suffering serious illnesses from time to time, and my grandfather with heart attacks, but death was something to which I had not given much thought. I think it was the manner of his death that impressed me. On the morning of that day, he had a slight heart attack, but by the afternoon he seemed to have recovered, and spent that time with me in the orchards as I cut the weed round the apple trees which were in full blossom. It was a glorious late April day, with the sun shining in a clear blue sky; the song of the birds and the hum of the bees made an idyllic setting.

My grandfather was not a man who expressed his emotions very often, but that afternoon as he quietly strolled among the trees he was whistling happily, something I had never heard him do before. There was a wonderful radiance in his face which impressed me, not knowing that he was near to death. That evening he seemed perfectly well, but before going to bed he asked my mother to wash his feet because, he said, 'I would not like to die with dirty feet.' That night he died in his sleep. At that time I was in the middle of my search for truth, and though it was to be several years before I reached what I believed to be my goal, my grandfather's approach to death was a great help to me.

Funerals in those days almost amounted to feasts. There would be a three course dinner for all who cared to come, after which the cortège set off for the church. Everyone walked, of course, and the coffin was carried by hand; in some instances for a distance of as much as four or five miles. I have seen as many as one hundred men walking in pairs in front of the coffin, and in front of them the 'time keeper' would walk. His job was to see that the leading four men stood out from the procession every minute, and waited, two on either side, until the coffin came abreast of them, when they took over the carrying until they reached the next four men.

Deep black was worn at every funeral — the ladies being heavily veiled, while the men wore bowler hats. Some of these hats looked a little tattered and some rather green with age, funerals being the only occasion on which they were worn. As the procession reached the church, the 'minute' bell would boom out from the tower. After the service my grandfather was laid to rest by six of his closest farming friends, in that part of the churchyard where his ancestors had been buried for three hundred years. As was the custom, relatives, friends and neighbours went back to our home after the burial, where another feast was laid out. Then it was back to the normal work of the farm. Life had to go on: the cows had to be milked and the stock fed, no matter what else happened.

After my grandfather's death, Polly and the jingle were hardly ever used; in fact, Polly spent almost every summer at Hartland Abbey, where the Dowager Lady Stucley, who was then well advanced in years, could depend on Polly taking her safely around in her four wheeled carriage. In 1932 the motor car arrived at Newton and made our transport problems much easier.

Some years before this, another modern invention had come to our home and opened up an entirely new vista of life for us. My mother's brother was what was then called a 'wireless engineer', and he had made a receiver for us. It was a huge box some two feet square with several valves and wires that always seemed to be getting disconnected. It usually happened when something important was to be heard, and we had to quickly run for the soldering iron in order to continue listening to the programme. This 'magic box', or so it seemed to us, was a great attraction for our neighbours who came evening after evening to listen with awe to what came out of it.

11

A New Family Begins

So I reached the magical age of twenty one — a year that was to be a very real milestone in my life. Up to that time I had had very little interest in the opposite sex, possibly because I had been too busy at work and at play. I had many casual acquaintances among girls, many whom I had gone to school and grown up with; others I had met at dances, and some always travelled with our band wherever we went. On one such occasion that year, a party of girls got on our bus at Clovelly, and a tall, beautiful young lady sat down in a vacant seat beside me. I had not noticed her at any previous dances, although it transpired that she had been to many. I had met my life's partner.

Dorothy lived four miles from my home, and immediately after our first meeting we began to go for long walks and sometimes cycle rides on Sunday evenings. We discovered that we had a great many common interests, such as music, and a love of nature, people and beautiful old houses and antiques.

She had not been so fortunate as I in her home life; her mother had died when Dorothy was only fourteen years old and from that time she had looked after her father and brought up four younger brothers.

The next two years gave us both such joy as we came to know each other and during the latter part of that time, to plan our future lives together. Dorothy came from a farming background, so it was not difficult for her to share my thoughts on that way of life. It was decided that when we married we should live in our little cottage of St Leonards, attached to our farm, where Jim Peard had lived up to the time of his death. It was a lovely, old-world, thatched three-bedroomed house, with a nice view across our farm. We had no modern conveniences; the toilet was outside and all the water had to be carried from a tap some fifty yards down the road. The cooking was done on a sturdy old bodley, but by this time life had been made more tolerable by the invention of the paraffin stove.

Dorothy and I spent all our spare time during the early months of 1934 decorating the inside of the house until it was ready for us to move in. It was then that difficulties arose: from where was the money coming to furnish it? We decided that we wished to be independent of family help if possible. I had not received any wages during all those years working on the farm. This was also true of most of my contemporaries on their farms. We caught rabbits from time to time and sold them for pocket money. Some of us kept a few hens and sold their eggs, or were given a ewe and sold her lambs when they were fat. None of us expected wages; we took it for granted that when we wished to marry, either we would live in a cottage on the farm or in part of the farmhouse and go into partnership with our father; or we would rent a small farm in the area and be set up with a few head of livestock and some implements.

So with a little of what we had been able to save in this way, we set off for the second-hand sales at Bideford. We were able to buy enough to furnish our cottage with the bare necessities for only £10, and with this, plus our wedding presents, we made a very comfortable home.

April 4th, 1934 dawned bright and clear with the promise of a balmy spring day. Our marriage was planned for eleven o'clock in the morning, but before that time there was much to be done; the usual morning's work with the livestock had to be completed before we could think about dressing for the service. But it was not long before we were in the vestry of the parish church, putting our signatures in those old registers where my forebears had done the same for many years. So with the blessing of my dear friend and vicar, we set out on the great adventure of married life.

My father had never enjoyed good health and a year after our marriage, on the advice of his doctor, he decided to give up farming and take a hotel at Westward Ho! At the same time my brother decided to go to London to work with an aunt who was a canine vet and this meant that I was left to run the farm alone, with the help of employed labour. The farm and the hotel were run as a joint enterprise, with the farm supplying eggs, butter, cream, and so on.

So it was that after just sixteen months of marriage we had to move out of our comfortable little cottage into the farmhouse. But before this we had a great disappointment. Our first baby was born, but due to a very difficult delivery she was injured at birth and lived for only one hour. Dorothy, too, was very ill for some time. Because the baby had died without being baptised, there was no burial service, so I gently wrapped her in cotton wool and placed her in a shoebox, which I strapped to the carrier of my bicycle and rode to the churchyard, where the sexton, George Vanstone, had prepared a little grave.

In this I laid her, commending her to God's care, and with the prayer that out of seeming disaster, Divine adjustment would ultimately be manifested.

It was good to be on our own at the farm and we soon settled down to managing despite difficult conditions. The only labour I had was that of Sam Babb who came to live in our little cottage, plus the part-time help of Jack Jeffrey. It was at this time, the early thirties, that the economics of farming became more difficult than they had ever been during my lifetime. Due to general inflation and high unemployment, the demand for our produce declined considerably, while our costs rose steeply. Manures, seeds, implements, rents and wages all cost more. A man's wage at that time was thirty-two shillings and six pence per week, which may seem very little compared to today's standards, but to reach that there had been a 50 per cent rise in ten years. To cope with these problems I had to change my methods of farming and along with many other farmers I switched from beef production to milk. This was collected each day and taken to a factory at Torrington which had been built a few years earlier as a cream processing plant. During the pre-war period, selling milk saved many farmers from bankruptcy.

Another important change took place on our farm at this time. The years had taken their toll of my beloved team of horses, Blossom and Jessie. They were getting too old to cope with the increased workload placed on them by the greater production on the farm, so they retired and a year or two later were 'put down' in order that they should not fall into other hands where they might be ill-treated, get into a bog on the farm or some such trouble as old horses sometimes did. Losing those two faithful creatures was as hard as losing a well loved friend.

As the horses passed out, the tractor moved in. Never again would Newton know that wonderful peace that had been its lot for so many centuries. Now the din of engines could be heard from almost every point on the farm, and from other farms as well. The wild life must have wondered what was disturbing their natural peace. The only creatures that seemed not to mind were the seagulls; they continued to follow the plough drawn by the tractor, just as they had done when the horses were doing the work; the only difference being that one no longer heard their squawking above the noise of the tractor engine. Neither, unfortunately, did one hear those other more pleasant sounds which were once a part of the ploughing scene.

The changes on the farms were not confined to mechanisation. Most of us kept Devon cattle at that time, or Red Rubies as they are called. These were mainly beef producing cattle, and one would hardly ever see another breed in North Devon. When we turned to milk production a different type of cow was required. So it was that the Friesian and Ayrshire breeds made their appearance, much to the disgust of many of the older generation of farmers, who called these animals 'those coloured things'. Economics had brought them, and they were here to stay, and they certainly produced the extra milk we required. It was much the same with the sheep. Before 1928 it would be difficult to find a breed of sheep other than the Devon Longwool in our area. But because the public demanded a smaller joint of lamb or mutton, and because we, the farmers, needed to keep more sheep per acre of land, we changed to the smaller Devon Closewool, or in some cases using a Suffolk or similar breed of ram. Here, too, the change had come to stay.

Life in the pre-war years was not as peaceful and stable as it once had been. Farming was changing from a way of life into a business. This became even more disturbing for me when I began to have strange thoughts

— at least they seemed very strange to me at that time: that perhaps farming was not to be my life's work after all, and that God wanted me to do something different. I had no idea what it was and, at first, as these thoughts occurred very infrequently, I was able to dismiss them easily as being too silly to bother about. After all, I was a farmer, born into that life and living in a place of which I felt a part. What else could I do, anyway?

Dorothy and I enjoyed life to the full, even though the work was hard and I had to give up some of the hobbies I had enjoyed for so long. The last to go were the bands: we played at our final dance after exactly ten years of so much joy and fellowship. Most of us had married by then and had taken on greater responsibilities in our work, but the memories of those happy days will always remain with me.

Our two daughters, Pamela and Janet, were born in 1936 and 1937 respectively, and we became a real family. They were baptised in the old parish church by Prebendary Gregory, and their names were added to the baptismal registers which contained the names of so many of our family who had lived in the parish for so long.

The year 1938 dawned on what was to be the most traumatic year of my life to that date. My brother, who was by this time married, decided that he would like to come back into farming again. It was impossible at that time to get a living for two families out of a farm the size of Newton, and we could not afford to set him up on his own, so we decided to leave the old home and rent a larger farm near Holsworthy for all of us. This decision hurt me terribly. No longer would I be able to look up from my work in the fields and see Lundy Island away in the distance, with all its changing moods, and its weather forecasting signs which I followed so closely: 'Lundy high, sign of dry; Lundy plain, sign of rain' — how true those signs used to be. No longer would I be able to look around the parish with all the familiar names: 'Leigh, Newton and Ley, Ugworthy, Bugworthy, Kernstone and Quay: Berry, Marketdon and Down; Cheristowe, Pattard and Hartland Town' as we used to say when we were boys. The familiar roar of the ocean, which had always been so much a part of the sounds of my life, would no longer exist for me. We called this roar the 'ground-swell'. It was the heavy undercurrent out in the ocean, which, when it came from the west, assured us of fine weather, but when it came up from the Cornish coast, we knew it would rain before twenty-four hours had elapsed. But my greatest loss would be the fellowship of so many friends, many of whom had grown up with me and shared my school life. Not least in all this loss would be my beloved church and all that it meant to me.

All this may sound somewhat sentimental, but it appeared to me that I should be leaving behind a part of my very being. Perhaps it was because my roots were so deep in that parish: like transplanting an established tree, it takes a long time for its roots to grow again. At last the great break came and we found ourselves established on a two-hundred-and-fifty- acre farm along with my brother and his wife; we settled down to make the most of what was a not too happy situation, with two families in one house. My roots did sprout again, but not to any great depth; those odd thoughts I'd had became more and more persistent; and something seemed to tell me that I was only a sojourner in that new home. At that time I still dismissed those thoughts, and did not even share them with Dorothy because I thought them too silly and did not want to disturb her. But my spiritual development just then was such that the dismissal was not quite as firm as it had been a few years earlier; although I had no idea what it was leading to, I began to toy with these thoughts.

12

My Call to a New Way of Life

Our new farm had been very neglected; the land had been farmed in a reasonable way, but the hedges were in a bad condition. We set to work to rear as many head of stock as possible — almost twice the number we had been able to keep at Newton. At the same time, we increased the acreage of corn so as to have several tons over and above the needs of the livestock.

We were made very welcome by our new neighbours, who were most kind and helped us in many ways. This did much to relieve the sadness of leaving Hartland. I took a while to get used to the little parish church, but here again there was a warm welcome from the priest. There was a warm welcome, too, from the congregation who seemed pleased to have a new family in their midst.

Then in 1939 came the war and all the changes that it brought about. We were ordered to plough up many acres of old grassland — in common with most farmers — and this had to be done with a reduced labour force. This meant longer hours in the fields which, thankfully, was made easier by the wonderful weather we had for the next three years. Because of the difficulty of finding enough labour to carry out the work we were ordered to do, we had two refugees from Nazi Germany. One of these young men was from from East Germany and the other was a Czech. They were not at all satisfactory; they wanted the safety of England without being prepared to contribute much in return. They were expected to help on the farm in return for their board and lodging, plus a small wage. Their lack of experience — one was a medical student and the other a trainee watchmaker — prevented them from doing most jobs on the farm; in the time it took us to show them how to do certain jobs we could have done them ourselves. The problem was that they wanted to do as little as possible, so I'm afraid they did not stay with us very long.

Like many other people in country districts during the first year of the war, we had two young lads from London placed with us. Ken and Raymond Russell were eight and nine years old and they had been born in the slums of Battersea. They had never been on a farm so their excitement was without bounds when they found themselves in the country with all the animals and the freedom to run and play. But like many of their contemporaries, when the novelty wore off they longed for the streets of London. However, their homesickness did not last for very long, and they soon settled into the country way of life, even to the extent of losing some of their cockney accent and acquiring a broad Devon dialect. They were dear boys and we missed them considerably when at last they returned to a more peaceful London.

During 1942 another important change took place in our lives. My parents' hotel was requisitioned by the military, so along with my brother and his wife, they rented another farm on the same estate, some three miles away. We divided everything in the way of livestock and implements, and started afresh, but with reduced labour and capital. The one great joy that came out of this was that Dorothy and I and our two children were alone again as a family.

The labour problem became acute for us now, and it was with some misgivings that we decided to have two Italian prisoners of war to work for us. These men were in a camp close to our farm and were allowed to live with us as a family. They proved to be very good workers, though a little temperamental at times. This was understandable considering their circumstances: they had received no letters nor heard anything of their home and loved ones for more than a year. They were kind and gentle young men, especially with the children. They became very angry with Dorothy when one of the children was smacked. The pair stayed with us for nearly two years before being replaced by German prisoners. These men were quite different from the Italians, having a temperament more like our own. They were even better workers, and often had to be told when to stop work. We became very attached to these, and I owe a great deal to them for their kindness and friendship during their stay with us.

During those war years we witnessed the bombing of Plymouth, even though that city was thirty miles away. The enemy planes seemed to begin their bombing run immediately above us; we could hear them turning and in a few minutes there was the sound of a distant explosion and the sky glowed more brightly on the horizon as that beautiful city burnt. One felt so helpless, and could only uphold those who were suffering and ask God's forgiveness for those who were causing such heartache and destruction. I well remember standing in our lane that night along with the two German lads, and we talked of the utter waste and futility of war. There was no bitterness in the hearts of those young men; they had long since learnt the folly of the teaching which had been inculcated into their minds since childhood — that war was a glorious thing. They knew, too, that what they saw happening to Plymouth that night, was also happening to their own beloved country. I think we all shed a few tears that night at man's inhumanity to man.

During 1942 a strange incident happened which was to have a very definite influence upon my life in later years. Our elder daughter, Pamela, had just started school, which she enjoyed immensely, but her mother found it difficult to get her to go to sleep each night. She wanted to stay awake and talk about school, with the result that the next morning she would be very tired. In desperation Dorothy sought my help: 'See if you can get her to sleep,' she said. I don't know what I did, but I simply smoothed Pamela's forehead and quietly said, 'You are going to sleep now, Pam.' I repeated those same words three or four times, and within a few minutes she was in a deep sleep.

I thought nothing more of it, except to say to Dorothy when I came down into the kitchen, 'It takes a dad to put the children to sleep.' Next morning when she went to call Pam for school, Dorothy was unable to wake her. She shook her arm, saying, 'It's time to get up, Pam', but there was no response. Dorothy realised that the child was still in a deep sleep, breathing easily, but with no sign of waking. She came down to me somewhat disturbed, suggesting that I should try to wake her. Again as on the previous evening, and for reasons of which I knew nothing, I did not try to wake her in the usual way, but simply said, two or three times, 'Pam, you are going to wake now.' The child opened her eyes, stretched her arms and got out of bed, quite refreshed and happy.

Again I thought nothing of it, except to ask my doctor a few weeks later why this child was so difficult to awaken in the morning after I had put her to sleep the previous night. He did not answer my question, but asked me how I had put her to sleep. When I told him, he said, 'There is your answer: you hypnotised her.' His suggestion of hypnosis troubled me somewhat at the time. I knew nothing whatsoever about it, only that it was some strange black art, and the hypnotist was a sinister Svengali type, using his evil power to impose his will upon his innocent victims. It was not until some years later that I was to learn how wrong I had been in my understanding of hypnosis, and to appreciate the marvellous gift with which God had endowed me.

I worked hard and long hours at that time. I had no hobbies, but longed for my music, so when I was invited to join a local concert party, I accepted gladly. Once again I got to work on my saxophone and thoroughly enjoyed the occasional outings.

In 1944 Dorothy presented me with a son whom we called William — a name that had been used in our family all down the centuries. This created another dilemma in my mind. Throughout the years of the war, my strange thoughts, which by now I shared with Dorothy, grew more and more persistent and took a more definite line. I became absolutely certain that God was calling me to be a priest. But I now had a son who would almost certainly want to be a farmer, as I had done and my family before me. What I found hard to accept was the fact that if I broke with tradition I would deny my son the opportunity to follow a way of life that had meant so much to me.

Despite my conviction that I was being called to the priesthood, I still fought God at every opportunity, using my love of farming and my hopes for my son's future as excuses. I even went so far as to seek to dedicate my farming to God's glory, and to serve Him in that way. I also used my lack of education as an excuse, suggesting to myself and to God that it would be impossible for me to be an efficient priest in those circumstances. Then it was that I hit upon what I considered to be a good way out of this dilemma: I would offer myself as a lay reader in the church.

Here I would like to pay tribute to the Reverend John Mayer, rector of the parish of Tetcott, where we later went to live, with whose encouragement, help and love I became a lay reader. I have often thought since that time, that John knew in the back of his mind this was only a stepping stone for me. My dear Prebendary, too, back in Hartland, did so much to encourage me.

At last I made the great decision, said farewell to my wonderful way of life and turned my face to the unknown. Immediately on making that decision I experienced the most wonderful sense of peace. For ten years I had fought God, but now nothing troubled me furthur. I just let go and let Him take over, which proved to be the greatest lesson of my life.

We went to live in a little cottage attached to my brother's farm where I could work for him and earn enough to keep us while I did my training. I could not afford to go to university for the full three years and at the same time maintain my family, so I decided to do my General Ordination Examination through a correspondence course, while carrying on my work on the farm. This took me six years to complete and I found it rather heavy going at times, especially during the busy summer months. I often did not get home until around ten o'clock on some evenings; then Dorothy would make me a jug of strong coffee and go to bed herself, leaving me to get down to biblical history, Christian ethics and all that was involved in such a course.

On Sundays I helped John Mayer, first by assisting him at services, and later by taking morning and evening prayer for him, when he had an additional parish placed in his care. Here, too, he was such a help to me, especially when I sometimes had doubts about being able to make the grade. I became aware also of the deep debt of gratitude I owed to Prebendary Gregory, not only for his teaching in my young days, but for his guidance and love. I shall never forget his joy when I told him of my decision to become a priest. He was so thrilled, he said, to think that one of his people, whose parents he had married and whom he had baptised, prepared for confirmation, married, and whose children he had also baptised, should be taking this step. I remember, too, the pleasure that was mine when he invited me to preach at my old church for Harvest Festival, while I was still a lay reader. Unfortunately he did not live to see me ordained. He died just two years before, after being vicar of Hartland for forty-two years.

It was at this time that our elder daughter Pamela decided to marry Bill Prouse at our little parish church, and the ceremony was conducted by John Mayer. When one's first child marries, it is a reminder of how quickly the years are slipping away: it seemed such a short time since her birth. Pam and Bill settled happily in their little cottage in the village, and Bill worked on my brother's farm.

As I came up to my final exams, it was necessary to be interviewed by the Bishop and his examining chaplain. Bishop Wilfred Westhall it was who welcomed Dorothy and me and our son to the bishop's palace at Exeter, and who did so much to make us feel at ease. I came to know him well in later years, and always felt wonderfully privileged to have been in the presence of such a saintly man. The bishop decided that I should spend one year at King's College, London, before being ordained a deacon. That year would be spent with the post-graduates of King's at St

Boniface College at Warminster in Wiltshire.

Before going to Warminster, arrangements had to be made for the welfare of Dorothy and our son Bill, who was ten years old by that time. Both our girls had left home: Pam was married and Janet was working with her favourite animals — a herd of cows in East Devon. Dorothy decided that she would like to spend that year as a housekeeper to a priest, where she could learn something of what life in a vicarage might be like before taking on that responsibility later. We put an advertisement in a church newspaper, the result of which was that one day we set off for the extreme boundary of the diocese of Exeter, to the little village of Holcombe Rogus, for an interview with the vicar of that parish.

It was from that time that I began to realise how completely God was taking over my life, now that I was prepared to drop all of my own ideas and let His will be done. It was the case in seeking this position for Dorothy; we were prepared to go wherever He desired us, knowing that it would be right, and the moment we arrived at the vicarage and met the Reverend John Adams, we knew this was the place for us. Mr Adams was a widower who had the care of two parishes and lived alone in a rather nice vicarage. His only help was a Mrs Hitchcock who came in each morning, so he needed a companion/housekeeper who could also help him entertain his friends. It was agreed that we should make his vicarage our home for the next year — a home to which I could come during vacations — and Dorothy would be paid one pound each week. During the weeks that followed our visit to Holcombe Rogus, we made arrangements to have our small amount of furniture stored, and finalised the details of my entry to King's. Then we made our farewells to new-found friends at Tetcott, this time cutting completely the line that attached us to our old way of life on the land, and turned our faces to the new life ahead — exactly twenty years after our marriage.

Part Two

13

Early Days in the Ministry

I was able to stay at our new home for a few days to see Dorothy and Bill settled in, before going on to Warminster. We found our first impression of Mr Adams to be more than justified; he proved to be one of the kindest men we had ever met, giving us completely free use of his house. He was good to Bill and made us feel that we had come to a home from home. This helped a great deal to alleviate the sadness of having to leave my loved ones as I set off for my final training year at King's. I had anticipated that I should be thrown in among fifty or sixty young men who had spent their whole lives in study, and who would not have much patience with a forty-two-year-old with my background. I was proved to be utterly and completely wrong. I discovered there were two other older men in my year; this gave me joy and did so much to boost my confidence. But the young men of around twenty-two years old went out of their way to make me welcome, and were themselves eager to share my experiences of life. They will never know how much they helped me.

St Boniface College, Warminster had been for many years a missionary training college until it was taken over by King's College, London. Here the ordinands in their final year could complete their training by doing some of the more practical work of a priest's ministry. We were sent out in pairs each Sunday to various little churches in the area, where one of us took the service, and the other preached the sermon. I sometimes felt sorry for those congregations who had to endure our amateurish attempts at conducting services, and listen to sermons which were often way above their heads, as it were; I know that many of those young men have since learnt to speak in a way that ordinary people can understand, and have come down to earth. I found this part of my training to be the least difficult, due to the fact that John Mayer and I had spent many hours together as he prepared me to become a lay reader. Another part of the curriculum I enjoyed was going into the local schools to teach religious education.

The college was a lovely old Victorian house on the main Warminster to Bath road, and I was allocated a bedroom-cum-study on the third floor. It was on my birthday that I began what was for me, literally, a new birth, a new way of life. It took several days for me, on waking in the morning, to accept the fact that I had no stock to feed and I often found myself looking at the sky and trying to assess what the weather was likely to be for that day. In fact, on my free afternoons I often walked along the roads out of the town, just to see what the farmers were doing. But little by little I settled into the routine of the college and began to enjoy my life. There was only one other man from the diocese in my year: Stanley Padgham from Plymouth. He, too, was a man of my age group who had been a stipendiary reader before offering himself for ordination. He found the pace even more difficult to cope with than I did and would often come into my room late at night, doubting if he would ever make the grade.

The warden was the Reverend Sidney Evans who later became Dean of King's, and is now Dean of Salisbury. The college chaplain was the Reverend John Townrow and the assistant chaplain Brother Timothy, BGS. The Dean of King's, the Reverend Eric Abbott, came down from London to spend each weekend with us. He later became Dean of Westminster. To all these men I would say a sincere 'thank you' for all they did to help a raw country bumpkin while he was with them for that year, and especially to the Dean, for his encouragement and brotherly support during our many walks together.

The college chapel was the focal point of our year together. It was there that we began each day with morning prayer at 7.30, and ended it with compline at 9.30 pm. This was especially exciting for me, never before having had such an opportunity for devotional worship. I found the emphasis on meditation to be wonderfully uplifting. We all greatly valued the Dean's Friday evening addresses which were tremendously inspiring, and did so much to help me.

The greatest difficulty I had when I first arrived at the college was getting accustomed to a way of worship that was completely foreign to me. I had been brought up in a fairly evangelical tradition, where ceremonial had very little place at the Eucharist, so I found it very strange at first, and even though I conformed to their tradition, it was rather galling at times and distracted me in my worship. I also found the lectures difficult to cope with at first, because I tried to take down too much detail, but I soon learnt the art of noting the relevant parts. Once each week we discussed a sermon, written by each of us in turn throughout the year. This was exciting until it came to one's own turn to stand up in front of the whole college and staff and read the sermon, and then have it torn to shreds, but it taught me a great deal about the art of preaching.

Almost every week one or more lecturers from outside the college would come to talk to us on various aspects of work in the Church. One such was the Reverend Jim Wilson of the Guild of Health, who, although he was with us for just two hours, made an impression on me that laid the foundation for my future work in the Ministry, though of course I was not aware of that fact at the time. I had from an early age been instinctively drawn towards people who were ill, or who were in deep trouble, and this was especially so with depressives. I had been fascinated by the processes by which humans, animals and the whole of Nature was continually being restored. I had studied Christian Science at some depth, and though I could accept a great deal of its teaching, there appeared to be a missing link, and this is what Jim Wilson seemed to provide for me.

In its denial of human aid in God's work of healing, I felt that Christian Science was putting that work on a magical level. I had seen in my work with animals and plants how necessary it is to co-operate with God, or with Nature as some would put it, if there was to be healing. At the human level this co-operation is all the more necessary because we have the power of choice and so often we prevent God from doing what is His perfect will, that is, wholeness for all His creation, by wrong thinking and action. Jim showed me that although God alone heals, He needs our co-operation in that work of healing, and that healing must mean wholeness of body, mind and spirit. Jim reminded me of the lines, 'Without God, we cannot. Without us, God will not.'

I very much enjoyed the seminars which were held weekly. It was here that we could share each other's thoughts and ideas, which helped me so much. There was supposed to be a strict silence after compline each night, but two or three of us would often sit in one of our rooms, drinking coffee and talking into the small hours of the morning. Here again, I gained so much insight into a world that had hitherto been hidden from me. But it was not all one-sided. Those lads were equally eager to share my experiences of life, especially those who had been brought up in a city environment and who knew that they might well find themselves with a group of country parishes to care for at some time in the future.

It was not all work at Warminster. Lack of

exercise was something that troubled me at first; a stroll around the lawn after breakfast before studies began seemed to be all that most of the men needed. But it was not sufficient for me after the active life I had known. We had every afternoon free until 4 pm, so I learnt to play golf. This got me away from the town to the top of Salisbury Plain with its wonderful views and lovely golf course. Here I could see the countryside for many miles, especially away to the west. Nostalgia would overwhelm me at times as I gazed in the direction of my old home and I wondered what I was doing in a strange county.

Time passed very quickly and it was not long before I was back with my family at Holcombe for my first vacation. It was Christmas, the first one we were not able to share as a whole family. I found that Dorothy had been coping very well in her new life but she had been rather lonely. Mr Adams decided to take a holiday as soon as I returned home, so we had the whole house to ourselves for three weeks, which gave us great joy, especially as one of our daughters was able to be with us. I enjoyed taking the services in the vicar's absence, but at that time he had to engage a priest to celebrate the Holy Communion.

The next term at college included Lent and Easter, which again was a wonderful experience. I especially enjoyed the retreats we had each term, when I was able to spend long periods in silence and felt very close to God, as I had been able to do as a farmer while working in the fields. This meant a great deal to me. I could never understand why some of those lads found it so difficult to be quiet, and were always doing something, or talking. I was greatly troubled about some of the young men because they did not seem to know God as a living, dynamic, divine consciousness, 'closer than breathing, nearer than hands and feet', as I knew him to be. Some of them just disappeared from the college, literally overnight, obviously being unable or unwilling to go any furthur in that direction.

During the next vacation, the one before ordination, it was the custom for the bishop of one's diocese to offer the ordinand a 'title', that is, a parish in which he would serve his first year as a deacon, under a parish priest whom the bishop thought to be suitable to continue a man's training after leaving college.

My diocesan bishop, Dr Robert Mortimer, suggested that I should go to South Molton, on the edge of Exmoor, and after much thought and prayer, I set off to meet the vicar of that parish. I was received most cordially and told about the kind of services held in that church, the type of people to whom I would be expected to minister, and the work I would be asked to do.

I boarded the train again for home, with all this information to share with Dorothy, but on that journey I became convinced that I should not be an assistant curate at South Molton. I could give no reason for this thought; in fact, if I had based my decision on the facts as they existed at South Molton, then I should have gone there. But some deep and overpowering conviction guided me to refuse the bishop's offer, and after talking it over with Dorothy, I wrote to him in that vein. The bishop's reply was to suggest that I go and see the Vicar of Dawlish. This time Dorothy went with me and we were met with the same hospitality and kindness as I had found at South Molton — in fact, the conditions in both parishes were almost identical, except that at Dawlish there was the added attraction of a beautiful little house overlooking the bay, which would be our home. Surely, we thought, this must be right for us. Then quite clearly and without any doubt at all, I knew it was not to be. So again, and this time with some trepidation, I had to tell my bishop that I could not accept his offer. He was most kind and understanding about it, and merely remarked, 'You are hard to please.' I explained that I felt it would not be good either for myself or for the people whom I would seek to serve if I was in the wrong place.

Time was getting short; I had come to the last day of my vacation, and still I had no title. We were sitting at lunch when the phone rang and was answered by Mr Adams, who came back to say that the Rector of Tiverton needed an assistant curate. We had to act quickly, and because Tiverton was not far from Holcombe, Mr Adams kindly offered to drive us to see the Reverend Canon R.C. Worsley that very afternoon. I had not been in his company for more than five minutes when I knew that this was the place for me to begin my ministry. The bishop was pleased to agree with our arrangements, so we went back to Holcombe having got over another hurdle; I then began to prepare to return to college for the last time.

It was agreed that after ordination we should live in a two-bedroomed flat on the second floor of the rectory while a house was made ready for us. I later found this close contact with my rector to be of great value. I had more opportunities of talking with him than would have been the case if I were living at a distance. I had kept bees since the age of eleven, and grown very attached to them, so I was able to continue that hobby, as well as sharing his gardening problems on my free day. We had our furniture taken out of store and installed in our little flat, ready for our occupation after ordination.

The last term was a short one, and was mainly taken up with the practical side of the deacon's work and ministry. At last we had our final interview with the dean, and having received his blessing, we made our farewells. We were to be scattered throughout the country from Inverness in the north to St Austell in the south, and to all kinds and types of parishes. So we went back to our home dioceses, to our ordination retreats. Our training was finished: now we had to begin to learn how to become priests.

My ordination retreat in the Exeter diocese was held at the convent of the Franciscan Servants of Jesus and Mary. Here again, I was introduced to a way of life that was completely unknown to me, and I realised that I had so much to learn from the practices of these dear people. I was greatly helped by the talks given by the bishop's examining chaplain, and even more so by the many opportunities for silence. It was good to have

Stanley from college days with me; we were the only two from King's to be made deacons at that ordination.

On the Saturday before the great day, we went to the cathedral for a rehearsal, and were shocked to learn that the service was to be televised — the first time an ordination had been on the screen. The rehearsal seemed to be quite a shambles, and we hoped that all would go well for the next day.

Trinity Sunday 1955 dawned with the promise of a perfect June day. After morning prayer we set off for the cathedral to arrive for nine o'clock, all adorned in our new clerical collars and cassocks. The day for which I had prepared for so long had arrived. That morning seemed a long way from my farming days in the old home at Hartland. I could hardly believe that I was not dreaming, and felt that I would wake to find myself working in the fields at Newton. The service began exactly at nine-thirty and was not concluded until half past twelve. I was glad that my family could be present, along with many friends from the old days; other friends were watching on television, but added to the warmth of that June day, the television lights made the heat in the cathedral very trying and the fact that the service was televised spoilt the day for me. We had to concentrate so closely on where we were standing at any given time, to be in the right spot for the cameras, that our thoughts were distracted from the importance of what we were doing. But nothing could spoil the reality of the moment when the bishop laid his hands upon my head, with the words, 'Take thou authority to execute the office of a deacon in the Church of God committed unto thee; in the Name of the Father, and of the Son, and of the Holy Ghost. Amen'; and when he handed me a copy of the New Testament with the words. 'Take thou authority to read the Gospel in the Church of God, and to preach the same, if thou be thereto licensed by the bishop himself.'

After the service we met for a celebration family lunch, and everything seemed to have changed, not only for me, but for my family as well. There were a lot of tears from the girls, although I am sure they were tears of joy.

John Mayer had by this time moved to a parish in Exeter, and he invited me to preach my first sermon in the diaconate at his church in the evening. This I was happy to do as a token of thanksgiving for all that John had done for me, and afterwards we set off for our new home in Tiverton. This was the first time that Dorothy and I had been alone since I left her for the ordination retreat, and as we climbed the stairs to our little flat we paused in the doorway, and I know we were both thinking the same thought, 'What have we done?' All the agonised thoughts of the years past; the hours of prayer and all the preparation passed through our minds, and in a moment of quiet we committed ourselves afresh to God.

Then we stepped inside the flat to a welcome that reduced us both to tears. We found huge boxes containing everything we might need for weeks to come: food, household goods and most lovely letters of welcome from the parishioners of St Peter's Church, and from the rector and Mrs Worsley. If ever there were two saints on this earth, they were Robert and Dora Worsley. Nothing was ever too much trouble for them when someone needed help. Everyone loved them and they were so humble and unassuming.

14

A Priest Is Born

So we settled into our new home and new way of life. Bill had to change schools for the second time in a year, which he did with remarkable ease considering his rather shy disposition. We quickly came to love the Worsleys and Dorothy was soon sharing with Mrs Worsley in the work of the Mothers' Union and the other parish organisations which a parson's wife is expected to lead.

I began my ministry, as is appropriate, at morning prayer in church at 8 am and ended the day with evening prayer at 5.30 pm. This is the pattern every priest is ordered to follow by the Book of Common Prayer, to which he assents at his Institution to a parish; as a deacon it was my duty to be there also.

The Church of St Peter, Tiverton, is without doubt one of the most beautiful churches in the diocese of Exeter, seating about eleven hundred people. During the time I spent in that parish there was a choir of over forty voices, and a brilliant organist called Mr Faff. To be led in the singing of hymns and canticles by such a choir was a revelation to me. I had never before shared such joy in that kind of music, not having had a choir in my home church. The anthems, too, were superb, Sunday after Sunday, as were the special concerts they gave at various seasons of the Church's year.

Canon Worsley made quite sure that I did not go to the services on the Sunday following my arrival in the parish without first being introduced to as many people as possible. After long talks about his plans for the parish and my part in them, we visited each churchwarden in turn and then met the parochial church council socially one evening — an event I shall long remember with pleasure.

A large housing estate was being built to the south side of the parish and my job was to build a congregation in that area. There was no church there, of course, and up to that time everyone had gone to the parish church which was quite a long way away. So a wartime Nissen hut was requisitioned in which we held our services and Sunday schools. The Bishop planned to create what was then known as a conventional district in that area prior to it becoming a new parish and church. This was indeed an exciting prospect for me as well as for the people on the housing estate. A plot of land was 'earmarked' for the new church, and a fund begun to purchase the many things that would be needed to run the church efficiently once it was built. Before we began to operate on a regular basis at Cowleymore, that being the name of the new estate, I helped with the services at the parish church. I was pleased to be able to do that because it gave me the privilege of joining with my rector, to learn from him and be helped by his vast experience.

During my first year, Canon Worsley insisted I write my sermons out in full each week, and discuss them with him every Saturday evening. We normally met in his study at nine o'clock but instead of immediately getting down to the discussion, we talked and talked about so many things. Robert Worsley had a wonderful memory and a vast store of jokes which we shared on those Saturday evenings, sometimes until past ten o'clock. Dorothy would hear our laughter after she had gone to bed. Suddenly, on looking at his watch, he would say, 'Come, Pennington, we must go through your sermon, I've still not done mine yet.' His criticism was always so constructive and helpful, but sometimes, by the time he had finished, my sermon had to be re-written completely, which often took me until the early hours of Sunday morning. Occasionally, because I was so tired or it was very late, I did not change the sermon as he had suggested. When I gave that address the next morning at the parish church, he would sit in his stall at the foot of the pulpit, with his head in his hands, listening intently to every word I spoke, with just an occasional nod of his head to indicate his approval. But never once did he comment afterwards, even when he must have known I had not changed the sermon in the way he would have liked. He was always a thorough gentlemen.

After living in the flat at the rectory for six months we moved into a nice house quite near to the district where I worked. Here I was among the people I was to serve, though Dorothy missed the fellowship of the Worsleys. We moved just before Christmas and our financial prospects for the festive season were not very bright, having arrived in Tiverton with only the clothes we wore, and my pay was such that it was impossible to save any money. I had a chat with our son Bill a few days before Christmas, and explained to him that we had no money with which to buy presents, but that we looked forward to better things to come in the future. Then it was that the Lord acted as I have known Him to do on innumerable occasions in such circumstances. I was going out of the front door just two days before Christmas when I found an envelope on the mat containing twenty-five pounds. It seemed unbelievable that such a large sum of money could be ours. To this day I do not know from whom that money came, but I do know how very grateful we were to that person. We thanked God for the wonderful way in which he works through His servants.

We soon settled down to a regular routine of services in the Nissen hut on the new housing estate. I spent most of my days getting to know the people there, and welcoming new families as they moved in. A part of my work that I enjoyed as soon as I began my ministry was visiting the two hospitals in the town. I seemed to be drawn to those places; I think I spent more time in them than I should really have done.

The time soon came around for my ordination retreat, before being priested, as we call it. A year had passed since we had last met as ordinands, so there was a great deal to talk about before the retreat silence began. Some men had sad tales of unhappy relationships with their vicars; others had found it difficult to settle into their new way of life. But most, like myself, had found a great happiness during that year, and were eagerly looking forward to becoming priests, and being able to take full part in the work to which we believed we had been called.

It was such a relief to be able to participate in the service of the Ordering of Priests without the distractions of the television we had experienced a year before. It was a wonderful moment for me when the bishop, with his suffragans and other priests, laid their hands upon my head with the words, 'Receive the Holy Ghost for the office and work of a priest in the Church of God, now committed unto thee by the imposition of our hands. Whose sins thou dost forgive they are forgiven, and whose sins thou dost retain, they are retained. And be thou a faithful dispenser of the word of God, and of His holy sacraments; in the Name of the Father, and of the Son and of the Holy Ghost. Amen.' Then the bishop handed me a copy of the Bible, with the words, 'Take thou authority to preach the Word of God, and to minister the holy sacraments in the congregation, where thou shalt be lawfully appointed thereunto.'

I had attained my goal. It seemed at that moment as if the whole of my past was laid out before me. Beginning not with those first vague thoughts of ordination, but away beyond that time to my early teaching in Sunday school and church at Hartland. It was as if time had ceased to be, and that I was in the eternal Now — at one with everyone who had ever influenced my life — all gathered up in that ecstatic moment. I was a priest and I knew without doubt that in all that had gone before, God had been leading me, even from my earliest days.

I felt especially grateful to my parents that day; it was they who had given me the basis on which to build. I could not have been closer to my dear friend and vicar, Ivon Lancelot Gregory, that morning, if he had been standing at my side. I had sat at his feet for twenty-seven years. I felt very honoured, too, because he had told me that when I became a priest, I should be the only man born and brought up at Hartland to attain that office since 1474 — the last man to do this being Hugh Prust, who was eventually 'unfrocked' for reasons unknown.

I went home that day with Dorothy, to begin the work which God had called me to do, and I was radiantly happy and humbly thankful for the great honour He had bestowed upon me. I could now take a full part in the worshipping life of the Church. My great joy was that I could celebrate Holy Communion, not only in church, but also with the sick in their homes.

With my mother: the wall seemed very high, but the world beyond was even more frightening, apparently!

Learning to be a farmer's boy under my grandfather's guidance.

Faithful Abbess was my constant childhood companion.

The family at tea on the lawn, with my pal Nun the dog in attendance.

'Gardeners' at Hartland School 1924. A field was specially set aside for the children to grow vegetables.

Arriving at Hartland Quay by modern transport for a day at the seaside.

The lads of the Silver Star Dance Band with whom I shared so many happy hours during the years 1927 – 37.

All my life before me — a portrait at the age of 21 years.

Happy faces at a Sunday school party in the Nissen hut at Tiverton, 1956.

With my young friends the Tiverton Sea Cadets and their officers.

Dorothy and I with our first foster child, Mark, at Bradford where all our fostering began.

Two later foster children, Michele and Monique, as bridesmaids at the wedding of David, whom we had also fostered, at North Molton church.

Sharing my niece Eileen's joy at her wedding.

Opposite page Dorothy and I with our three children on our thirtieth wedding anniversary.

Baptisms are always happy occasions, even if Mum seems to have left me holding the baby!

15

Parish Life

Not long after being ordained a priest I gradually came to realise that it was in my ministry to the sick where I found the greatest satisfaction. This was not only in what was achieved, but rather in the 'oneness' with Christ that resulted from letting go of myself and becoming a channel for His work of wholeness. Time and time again I found that in bringing some poor soul into the sphere of Christ's healing touch I myself experienced a wonderful sense of nearness to the Lord. I would take that even further by saying that in becoming a channel in Christ for some sick person, His healing power quite often rubbed off, as it were, on to me either physically, mentally or spiritually.

One of my first joys after my ordination into the priesthood was the marriage of our younger daughter Janet to John Wright at the parish church. It proved to be a very emotional experience, but a happy one. To hear my own daughter making her marriage vows in front of me was very wonderful. The lovely prayer of blessing used at the end of the actual marriage seemed to be just what I wished to say to my children. 'God the Father, God the Son, God the Holy Ghost, bless, preserve and keep you: the Lord mercifully with His favour look upon you: and so fill you with all spiritual benediction and grace, that you may so live together in this life, that in the world to come you may have life everlasting.' To be able to speak those words in God's name to my own daughter was indeed a great joy.

We soon made many friends in Tiverton, and the months sped quickly by. I well remember the first baptism at which I officiated. It had been arranged that twelve babies should be baptised at the same time one Sunday afternoon. I had met some of the parents and godparents for the usual preparation talks, and the rector had seen the remainder. When I arrived at the font I found such a crowd of people that I had difficulty in sorting out who was who — parents, godparents or friends. At last I was able to get the necessary people in a semicircle round the font where I could speak to them, and hear their responses. The service went well for some ten minutes and then a baby began to cry. This triggered off eleven other little voices, and louder and louder they cried until my voice became almost inaudible to anyone in the church. I resolved, there and then, never again to take a mass baptism.

I had a similar experience at a mass wedding, though this time without crying babies. For some reason which I cannot remember, my rector had arranged for four couples to be married at one service. I had interviewed one couple and he the other three. At the sound of the Wedding March, four brides, each on the arm of their respective father and each followed by their bridesmaids, processed up the aisle, led by myself. By the time we reached the chancel steps, the four bridegrooms, along with their best men were standing in a row with their backs towards us. I had the awful thought: supposing one of the brides does not recognise the back view of her groom and stands beside the wrong man. When they were in their correct positions, I had to decide who were bridegrooms and who were the best men, so as not to put the questions to the wrong man. Of course, each couple was legally and correctly married separately, though much of the service was used for all together. Again I made the decision that this would not be repeated.

In building up the congregation for the new church and parish, a great deal of time was spent with children and young people and working with them has always given me much satisfaction. We had a wonderful Sunday school with six teachers, and a youth group of fifty members who belonged to the Anglican Young People's Association. These young people were all confirmed and formed a dynamic group in all kinds of Christian work. I well remember following the choir in the parish church from their vestry, up the aisle to the chancel for morning prayer one Sunday. As I passed by the seats, a shrill little voice said, 'Mummy, there's the man who knows about God.' I had been talking to his parents at their home, and Jeremy had obviously been listening.

Of all the variety of work that was mine as a priest — preaching, teaching, conducting services and visiting people in their homes and in hospital — the work which gradually came to give me the greatest satisfaction was my ministration to the sick, and especially the mentally sick with whom I developed a particular empathy. I had occasion to visit parishioners at the psychiatric hospital in Exeter from time to time and found myself becoming very attached to them. During my visits to that hospital, I came to know a Christian psychiatrist whose thinking about the Church's Ministry of Healing was very much in tune with my own. This relationship developed and I began visiting the hospital on a regular basis to seek help for patients he referred to me. This was the beginning of a part of my ministry that was to give me great satisfaction for many years.

It was not until I had been working with the mentally sick for a few years that I began to wonder why I was so much drawn to them and their needs. It may seem strange to some people, but the happiest days of my ministry have been spent with mentally disturbed people. As early in my life as I can remember, there was a man who lived quite close to our farm who suffered from manic depression, though I do not think it was recognised as such in those days. During his very bad times he would ride his little white pony at a terrific speed, seemingly straight at us children. He talked to himself a great deal while he knelt in the road and broke stones into powder with another stone. This must have required tremendous strength, and I often used to go to that spot after he had gone, and marvel at what he had done, while at the same time feeling an intense wave of sadness that a man who in his saner moments was of such a lovely disposition and a thorough gentlemen, could become so disturbed. I often visited his home with my family for a meal, and I can remember wondering even at that early age what it was that seemed to change him into a completely different person from the delightful host sitting opposite me at the table. I have come into contact with many similar cases since that time, and often my thoughts have gone back to that friend, now long since passed to his rest.

It was at this time, too, that I began to study hypnotherapy, remembering the wonderful gift that I had discovered many years before. I talked to Christian doctors and psychiatrists about the use of this therapy, and we came to the conclusion that because so many psychological problems have their foundation in the unconscious mind, until their causes have been identified and 'dug out', as it were, there can be no real and lasting healing. I have always used hypnotherapy in the context of prayer, seeing it as means of discovering the cause of certain symptoms, and then going on to create the conditions in a person's body, mind and spirit, in order that God may heal.

Very early in my ministry I discovered the evil of sickness brought about by unconfessed sin. During the course of my visiting in Tiverton, I met a lady who was so crippled by arthritis that she was completely helpless. She had to be carried from her bed and put in a chair each morning, and back to her bed at night. In talking to her I learnt that her husband had left her when their two daughters were aged four and five. Because of this action, she had built up a most terrible hatred against him. When she talked of what he had done, her features became distorted with anger and hatred, and she clenched her fists until her knuckles became white with the pressure, as though they were coming through her skin. Her limbs shook, as if out of control and I wondered if her arthritic condition had been caused, or perhaps made worse, by the hatred that had built up within her. I visited her weekly for several months, and each time we talked about the love and healing power of Christ, and our need to co-operate with Him in His desire for wholeness in our lives. Then we went on to talk of the fact that we ourselves often prevent Him from bringing healing into our lives and sometimes even bring sickness and disease upon ourselves by wrong thinking, and especially sinful thinking and action.

As the weeks went by, we looked together at her early years with her husband, and she admitted that she had often been the cause of some of the disagreements between them, so that she was partly to blame for the action he took. I suggested that she learn to love her husband, and ask for forgiveness for her part that led to the separation. This she did in a very real way, so much so that within a few weeks there was a decided improvement in her condition, her countenance became relaxed and a wonderful look of peace spread over her face. But even more than that, she used to say that she felt alive again. I went to see her just before I left that parish, and I found her walking with the aid of a frame. It may well be that she will never again find complete physical healing, but she found something more valuable — the attitude of mind and strength of purpose in Christ to overcome any disability, instead of allowing it rule her life.

I became very interested in the Sea Cadets while at Tiverton, and spent much time at their headquarters as their chaplain. It was such a joy to share with those lads in their varied activities, seeking to relate spiritual realities to their hopes and aspirations for their future: for many of them a career in the Royal Navy. It gave me great satisfaction, too, to see how much these young men were supported by their elders, and not least by prominent townspeople, including the mayor. Those lads were not slow in responding to that encouragement.

I shall always remember with gratitude the

wonderful help I received from my rector and friend, Robert Worsley. Not only did he help me with the ordinary mundane things, such as conducting services of all kinds, but out of his vast experience of parochial life, he shared with me many other thoughts. He used to say how important it was to know people; to know how to cope with difficult members of parochial church councils, Mothers' Unions and similar organisations, as well as in the ordinary round of visiting. I sometimes found it embarrassing during my first weeks in the parish to find myself preaching to a congregation of some five hundred people made up of a high proportion of well-educated people — doctors, solicitors and other professional types. I remarked to my rector that I felt somewhat inadequate because of my lack of a higher education. He paused for a moment and quietly replied, 'Pennington, that is pride.' How right he was. I had never before thought of inverted pride.

Another relationship I had to cultivate on coming into that parish was with the clergy of the Deanery. To be involved in a 'gaggle' of clergy, or whatever the right term might be, was something quite new to me. I was sometimes mystified by remarks made at the Chapter meetings and on other occasions. One found, for instance, clergy for whom robing in this way or that, at a service of Holy Communion, or of doing certain actions in a particular way had become almost an obsession. One priest went so far as to impress upon me the fact that unless a priest wore vestments, the Eucharist was invalid. The Book of Common Prayer states that these things shall be done 'decently and in order'. I have sought throughout my ministry to abide by the principle that I have no moral right to change the tradition of a parish by imposing my will. Those people who worship in a particular parish will, in all probability, still be worshipping there after I have left, as they were long before I came. I may not like surplice and stold, or vestments for Holy Communion, but if those parishioners prefer one or the other, then I have no right to change that preference.

Towards the end of my third year at Tiverton, I received an invitation from Eric Abbott, who was by then Warden of Keble College, to accept the 'living' of two parishes in the diocese of Bath and Wells, Upton with Skilgate, of which he was the patron. Naturally both Dorothy and I were thrilled at the idea, and also that my rector felt I was ready to take on the responsibility of a parish of my own. Our first step was to visit those parishes, to 'spy out the land' as it were. A churchwarden kindly showed us around. One of the churches was beautifully kept, while the other was in a terrible state. It was obvious that a lot of work was required in those parishes, which would have been a tremendous challenge to us. When shown the rectory we had a great surprise as it one of the most beautiful houses we had ever seen. It had a domed entrance hall with stained glass, from which seven doors opened into various rooms, one of which was a lovely private chapel set out in every possible detail.

My next move was to inform my own diocesan bishop of the offer that had been made to me. He replied in no uncertain terms, 'If Eric Abbott can offer you a living, so can I. Will you go and look at Bradford and Thornbury?' So having written to thank Eric for his kind offer, and explained the circumstances, we set off to explore the possibilities of the bishop's offer. It was almost like going home again, because Bradford and Thornbury were in the Deanery of Holsworthy in which we had lived for fourteen years before I went to Theological College, and where I had been a lay reader. In fact I had officiated at services at these churches and was known to many of the parishioners. The parishes had been vacant for about a year, several priests having been to look at them, but in each case they had turned down the bishop's offer because they thought the rectory at Bradford was too large.

This house was a beautiful example of Elizabethan architecture. It had nine bedrooms and an 'alms-hole' of that time. This was a tiny room from which the priest distributed the alms to the poor of the parish. The winding staircase was of polished oak, with the arms of Exeter cathedral and bishop's mitres carved in various places. A large window above the staircase was of stained glass, depicting saints and their crowns. There were also two large lawns, a garden and four acres of glebe land, with the most beautiful avenue of beech trees.

The great welcome we received from the churchwardens as they showed us the house and the two lovely little churches added to our first favourable impressions and we talked about all this at great length on arriving home in Tiverton. It was then that our enthusiasm came to be blunted by the fact that this would mean leaving so many dear friends with whom we had worked and played for three years. I am not sure whether it is just sentiment on our part, but we have always been terribly hurt when we have had to leave a parish; we seem to get so close to people that it is as if we leave part of ourselves behind when we move on. Leaving Tiverton was the first of those heart-rending experiences.

I accepted the bishop's offer, and with the blessing of my rector, we set about preparing to move. A great deal of redecorating had to be done in the house before it could be occupied, and this was done by a firm of builders whose director had become a close friend: Vic Broomfield and his wife Lorna were always so kind to us. Dorothy had to make the journey to the house once more to deal with curtains and carpets, but at last it was ready for our occupation. But there was still another side to the move to be arranged, and that was the ecclesiastical. I was wonderfully helped by a saintly man, for whom nothing was too much trouble, to make sure that my Institution and Induction into those parishes went smoothly. He was Canon Hall who was then Archdeacon of Totnes, and in whose archdeaconry were the parishes of Bradford and Thornbury. Not only did he tell me what I should do, he even went with me to see the registrar to make all the arrangements. I am indeed grateful to him.

When all the plans were completed for our move and reception into the parishes, then came my last service and the sad farewells. At that service we were presented with wonderful gifts, one of which touched us deeply because it was signed by all the young people of our congregation. When we came out of the Nissen hut in which we had shared so many happy hours in worship and fun, about a dozen teenage girls were leaning their heads against the wall, weeping bitterly. We had not stayed long enough to see the new church built, but we believed a good foundation had been laid for the congregation that would eventually use it. We are so grateful to those dear souls whose patience and love with a raw recruit in the ministry made it possible for him to learn so much. Here I would salute the memory of Robert Worsley with affection and gratitude, knowing that without his tolerance, kindness and encouragement, I should be the poorer today.

16

New Pastures

So we arrived in the new 'vineyard' to which we believed we had been called. There were three days before the Institution and Induction which gave us time to settle in our home and find our bearings. At last the great evening arrived when, in a crowded church, I made the necessary declarations, and my oaths of loyalty to the Queen and of obedience to the bishop, who, as I knelt before him, handed me my Seal of Office. Then followed my induction by Canon Hall, when I was led by the churchwardens, first to the door which I unlocked and where the archdeacon inducted me 'into the real, actual and corporal possession of the rectory and parish church, with all the rights, members and appurtenances thereto belonging'. Next I was taken to the tower where I tolled the bell to signify to the parishioners that I had been duly installed as their rector. There is a curious idea connected with this bell tolling; people say that the number of times the bell chimes indicates the number of years the priest will stay in that parish. I don't know how many times I rang it that evening, perhaps a dozen, and that would not be far off the number of years I stayed at Bradford and Thornbury.

We next went to the font, where I promised to prepare and bring all to be baptised. From there we went to the lectern, where I undertook to read the Word of God in a way that could be understood by the people. Finally we arrived at the altar, where in Christ's Name I would celebrate the Holy Communion. The archdeacon then led me by the hand to my stall, the symbol of my office, where I felt very humbled at the honour bestowed upon me, and thankful to God for bringing me along the road to that day.

I remember how concerned my brother was when he knew I was to become rector of those parishes and he asked if I felt sure I could cope. I could understand his feelings; what he did not realise was that I was not shouldering that burden alone, but that God, who had so wonderfully led and guided me all those years, would continue that support. Of that I was sure.

The first day of my ministry as a parish priest dawned as only a late May morning can, warm and balmy, and my joy that day was unbounded. After morning prayer in church at which I tolled the bell as I was commanded to do, Dorothy, our son Bill and I walked round the lawns, garden and fields. For Bill, who was by this time fourteen years of age, this was the first time he had been able to walk on fields other than those belonging to other people. Now he was free to come and go as he pleased, and it was as if some buried desire came to the surface of his mind. From his earliest years Bill had wanted only to be a farmer. He could not remember living on a farm, even though he had been born during my farming days, but it was as if the generations of his farming forebears influenced his future life. There and then he began to make plans to use the land and buildings.

For me that morning walk was a sentimental journey. I was back again, as in the old days, treading the soil that was so much a part of my nature. Those trees and hedges seemed especially beautiful on that glorious May morning and every blade of grass seemed to say, 'You have come home.' The lawns and gardens had been sadly neglected, but the Virginia creeper, with which the house was covered, was just coming into bud, and it was not difficult to imagine the riot of colour that autumn would bring.

My four churchwardens proved to be the most helpful, kindly men any parish priest could hope to have: John Cox and Les Parsons at Bradford, Jim Daniel and Tom Vanstone at Thornbury. John was the local postmaster, Les was a postman and farmer, while Jim was a blacksmith and Tom a farmer. During all the years I was with them there was never a harsh word spoken. They were a wonderful team.

The next step was to meet the two parochial church councils separately, to discuss the services and take a look at the finances of the parishes before settling down to a routine of visiting and getting to know the people. I soon realised there was a great deal to be done in both parishes. The congregations were pitifully small; there was no help being given to children at Sunday school, and both churches needed redecorating. The income from offerings and other sources was so low that there was no money to do anything other than pay our dues to the diocese — even that was not always possible. This might have seemed a daunting task were it not that I remembered Canon Worsley's advice, 'Don't jump in at the deep end; make haste slowly.' I later discovered that this was exactly right, and especially so because these were country parishes. There is nothing that upsets a countryman more than for a parish priest, or anyone else for that matter, to come into a parish and start at once to turn everything upside down. A remark one often hears on coming into a new parish is, 'Parson So-and-so never did this or that; he always did it in this way.' So for a few weeks I made sure I did nothing which was in too great a contrast to my predecessor. I soon realised, too, that it would have been much harder and less rewarding if I had come into those parishes with everything spick and span, and no changes needed.

I have always liked the word 'parson', and encouraged people to use it, although in Devon we say 'passon'. It is from the Latin *persona*, meaning person, and I like to think of the parson as being God's Person in the parish. The idea of the parish priest being called Father does not appeal to everyone, especially in the country parishes, where he is known as Passon So-and-so. It was not until I became a parish priest that I realised how close a parson and his people could be. He becomes involved not only in their intimate family and domestic problems and joys, but also in the wider secular and parochial organisations, such as the parish council, school managers and other committees in which he is expected to take a part. I believe it is right that he should be so involved, because it helps to overcome the misunderstanding which some people have, of seeing the Church as a building, and a priest's work as being confined to that building. My experience has shown me that many opportunities occur in a secular gathering for Christian witness, because one is often then in the company of people who would rarely, if ever, be seen in church.

This involvement on the part of the parish priest has the added effect of bringing him down from the pedestal on which people seem to put him, but one has at the same time to keep a correct balance. The 'hail fellow, well met' type of parson who goes around slapping everyone on the back is running the great risk of not being the priest or the teacher that he should be, but just one of the boys. One has to learn the art of enfolding one's people in one's arms, metaphorically speaking, while at the same time, gently keeping them at arm's length. I once knew a priest who encouraged his people to call him by his Christian name, children and adults alike; the result of which was that he had to leave his parish — he could not teach effectively any longer.

My first year in those parishes was spent in getting to know the people and starting a

Sunday school, as well as carrying out the normal tasks of a parish priest. Our lovely house soon became our home and we all loved it tremendously, but the garden and lawns were not so easily transformed; in fact, it took us almost two years to get them into some sort of order. Bill made good use of the land and sheds, and was soon deeply and enjoyably involved in breeding pigs, which he sold for fattening.

At the end of my first year I felt the time had come to get down to some real spadework in the parishes. The Mother's Union needed to be reorganised, having lapsed some years previously. Dorothy undertook this task with great success, thanks to the wonderful co-operation of the ladies of both parishes who rallied round us, not only in this effort, but in everything we did. A lot of travelling with the car had to be done before each meeting, to collect members over a scattered area, and bring them to the rectory, but it was time well spent. The branch continued to thrive all through our years there.

A way had to be found to encourage people to give a more realistic amount of their money back to God, and in so doing, to teach them how to give themselves through their time and their talents. The Bradford

Parochial Church Council decided to do this by embarking on a Christian stewardship campaign, so we sought the help of the Diocesan Adviser, who came and talked to us about the problems of such a venture, and helped us with literature.

The campaign involved many people over a period of a year or more. First a small group had to be trained to visit every home in the parish to explain the purpose of the operation. I well remember the first time I talked to this group about what was expected of them: they were unanimous in making it plain that they could never meet my expectations. As the weeks of training went by they became more confident, but were still conscious of their inadequacies. By the end of the six-week course, I had written to every home in the parish, explaining our objective, and saying that a member of the team would be visiting their home within the next two weeks. They were wonderful weeks for those five men. They had been commissioned at the Holy Communion service the previous Sunday and on the following evening, each having been allocated a number of homes, they set off to become evangelists for the Lord in a very real way.

I had listened to mock interviews during their training and I was amazed to hear those men, who only some six weeks previously had been so sure they could not do what I was asking of them, standing in front of their friends with such confidence. I heard them talking about the fact that we own nothing, but are stewards of God's gifts. They stressed that we should give back to Him a worthy proportion of that which He has loaned us. I was so thrilled that tears came to my eyes; I knew that God was going to use those faithful disciples well. After the visiting was completed, a number of ladies went to each home with an invitation to attend a parish supper, at which the bishop and his wife would be present, and where more information on the campaign would be given. This meal was a great success. The Rectory Room where all the parish functions were held and which used to be an old tithe barn was completely full and the ladies excelled themselves by putting on a marvellous meal. That night I felt that all our efforts had been well worth-while.

When the pledge cards which had been given away to every family began to come in, it was evident that people had accepted our challenge and were responding wholeheartedly. When the final financial results became available, we found that we were assured of a 400 per cent rise in our annual income; but more important still, the number of people who dedicated their time and talents by taking on all kinds of work for the Church was beyond our imagination. A thanksgiving service was a fitting end to what had been a memorable year for that parish. We had so much for which to thank God. Even that was not the end. As the months went by it became apparent that more and more people were attending church on a regular basis; people that previously only came on special occasions were to be seen in church week after week. Many young people came forward for confirmation — all this because a few faithful souls were prepared to allow God to use them and take them along unknown paths to work for Him.

Thornbury had its faithful characters, too: there was Mr Herbert Nile who came to church every Sunday, no matter what the weather might be, on his tricycle. He always wore breeches, with highly polished boots and leggings, and sat in the choir. Sam Skinner was a very small man who pumped the organ Sunday by Sunday, seemingly never absent. Two humble and simple characters who I am sure must have been 'God's little ones' as Jesus called such people.

17

My Developing Interest in the Ministry of Healing

After some two years at Bradford and Thornbury, Dorothy and I began to feel that we were not being stretched to our full capacity, and that there were areas in our lives that needed to be looked at. The first of these was our house with its nine bedrooms — only two of which were in use, so we decided to give holidays to deprived children. An organisation in Bristol undertook to cover the cost of their rail fares, and we did the best we could to give them an experience to remember.

All the children, who had never before had a holiday, came from very poor families. I remember one little boy who arrived wearing a jacket that was obviously his father's, with the sleeves reaching below his fingertips. For these little ones a visit to the seaside was something out of this world; one little lad stood on the cliff-top and gasped, 'My, what a lot of water.' I doubt if that old rectory had heard such shrieks of laughter echoing through its corridors for many a long year. We had our moments of frustration when these children, who had never before been outside their city boundaries, began to spread their wings during the first few days of their visit. One never knew what mischief they would be doing next — all of which was a great trial to Bill, because it was generally his animals with which they became involved. These children obviously enjoyed their holidays, but this was more than matched by the joy that was ours in seeing those little lives unfolding in the fresh air and the freedom of the countryside — something we took for granted.

After a while we felt that our home was still not being used to its fullest capacity, so we decided to foster children on a temporary basis. This would cover the whole year instead of just holiday times. Little did we think that when little Mark came to us he would be the first of forty-five who would share our home down the years. Mark's mum wished to do nursing training, and having no one to care for him during that time, he stayed with us for three years. Today he is a massive six-footer, but still calls us 'my other gran and grandad'.

The others came to us in all sizes and ages, from a few days to fourteen years, but they all brought with them their utter dependence and love. Some came while mum was in hospital, others because they had no home or had been abandoned by their parents. They came for varying lengths of time, from a few weeks to those who came to us at five months and are still with us, seventeen years later. Michael and David came to us at the age of seven and nine years, when their home broke up. I shall never forget the day Dorothy and I brought them to our home; they looked so broken and frightened — two little lives lost in a great big world, seemingly without love. Now, twenty-one years later, they are happily married — David having made a career for himself in the army. But we are still their 'gran and grandad'.

One cold, dark April evening four little people were brought to our home, aged from five months up to three and a half years. Their mother had been unable to cope, so André, Gina, Michelle and Monique became part of our family. André and Gina eventually went back to their mum, but Michelle and Monique are still with us. All our foster children up to that time had called us Gran and Grandad, but one evening just after Michelle and Monique had started school, they came home and asked if they could call us Mum and Dad. We felt they were very much ours from that time, and would have liked to adopt them, but this was not possible, even though they took our name. The love these little ones brought into our lives has been beyond measure.

Another development in our work was the reception into our home of teenage girls, aged from fourteen to sixteen, who had become pregnant, and had in some cases been turned out of their homes. We had twenty-two of these unfortunate, frightened young people down the years and shared with them some of their fears and frustrations. We came to know and love these girls during their four or five months' stay with us, and sought to uphold them when the time came for them to go home without their babies. Sometimes it took several months to complete the adoption arrangements, and when at last the helpless little one left our home it was as if one of our own children was being taken from us, and there were always a few tears.

Life in the parishes continued its relentless course: teaching, preaching, visiting the sick with Holy Communion and helping to resolve people's problems. Weddings and funerals — rejoicing with the happy ones; supporting those who were sad. Preparing young people for confirmation and couples for their marriage. Sharing with the dear souls committed to my care the changing ecclesiastical seasons of the year, as well as the changing seasons on the farms. All of which adds up to the joy and satisfaction of every parish priest. My interest in the Ministry of Healing had not diminished one little bit, in fact I increasingly found it to be of paramount importance if I was to do the work efficiently to which I believed I had been called.

A young wife and mother in one of the parishes, who often played the organ in church, had a serious mental breakdown. She had had similar experiences before, and gradually come out of them, though each had been worse than the previous one. Her psychiatrist doubted if she would recover from this particular attack. I visited her in the mental hospital, but was at first not allowed to see her because she was in such a disturbed state. Eventually the sister agreed to let me in to what was in those days a padded cell where the patients could not harm themselves. Mary did not recognise me and continued to rampage around the room which contained only a mattress on which she slept. At first she was extremely violent towards me, and I wondered if I should ever be able to help her. Gradually, as I upheld her in prayer, she became more quiet, and eventually I was able to get her to lie on her mattress. It was at this time that I had to make an important decision: was this girl possessed, or was she mentally ill? During those few minutes as she lay on that mattress I became overwhelmingly conscious that God was directing me to be a channel of healing for this beautiful young woman. I was so sure that His will for her was that she would be radiantly whole and completly free from this mental illness. I knelt beside her and laid my hands upon her head for several minutes, and at the same time knowing that God's healing love and power were being manifested in her whole being. It was then that I felt her body suddenly go limp, and for one awful moment I thought she had died. But I soon realised that she was asleep, and breathing as easily and lightly as a baby.

When I rang the bell for Sister to unlock the door, and told her that Mary was asleep, she did not believe me, saying that Mary had had no sleep without heavy sedation for several weeks. Sister could hardly believe her eyes when she looked at Mary, and after locking the door she promised to ring me later that evening. This she did, saying that when she visited Mary's room some time after I left she found her sitting on her mattress asking where she was and why she was there. Mary has had several worrying events in her life since that time, but with no recurrence of her illness, and she now lives a full and happy life. This incident further convinced me that Christ still heals as in the days of His flesh, and uses many kinds of channels for His work.

When people have problems or are in a depressive state, they are generally at their worst in the early hours of the morning. It is at that time I often get a call. I well remember one such journey on a dark and foggy night to a lovely family whom I knew well and where the mother had come to breaking point and was unable to cope. I am never at my best at one o'clock in the morning, after having had only about two hours' sleep and with the prospect of a drive of several miles ahead of me. On this occasion I remember I was especially tired after having had a heavy day previously, and I found it difficult to prepare myself, as I like to do, on the journey to the home.

When I arrived I found a situation like so many others I have encountered down the years. The children were in bed, thankfully oblivious to what was happening, while Mum sat in her chair in front of the fire, utterly and completely broken, with Dad doing his best to console her. These people were above average in intelligence, and at the same time were a loving, integrated family. Little did they know but that night was to be a turning point in their lives, when their whole way of life was to be changed. George, the husband, was a farmer, a kindly man who was prepared to help anyone in trouble. He was not a dynamic Christian in any sense; he went to church occasionally but it did not mean much to him. His wife, Joan, was a regular worshipper and someone to whom Christ was a reality.

We spent more than an hour together in conversation and prayer, and as I laid my hands upon her in healing prayer at the end of that time, I knew that God had taken over. George had been sitting at the opposite side of the room all this time, and when he saw the great change that took place in his wife when Christ took control, he broke down and wept. Joan was completely healed and began to live a full and radiant life. But it was on her husband that the Holy Spirit had the greatest influence. George was so impressed by what had happened to his wife that he sought every opportunity to come to know more deeply the reality of Christ. I passed him over to his parish priest, and some months later he was confirmed. But his conversion did not stop there; he became convinced that God wanted him to become a priest. In a few years, during which time he tested this call to the utmost, he found himself at a theological college and was eventually ordained a priest in the Church of Christ.

About this time the North Devon Coroner's report showed that there had been a gradual increase in the number of suicides in the area over the years. When the records of other centres of population were compared, it was found that we had the highest number of suicides per thousand head of the population than any area outside London. At a meeting of interested people, clergy and lay, it was decided to form a branch of the Samaritans, with an office which despairing and suicidal people could phone or visit. I felt that here was a very worth-while way of giving oneself to the needs of others. Most of those who go to the Samaritans simply wish to talk, either to a voice on the phone or to someone at the office, face to face, whom they can trust with their intimate problems. Many a time I have taken a call around two o'clock in the morning. It is at this time that many people feel their loneliness to be the most acute; or they may have lain awake until that time with their problem growing more and more menacing all the while. I have often lain in bed listening on the telephone to a sad story for anything up to two hours. They would then apologise for keeping me from sleep for so long, and thank me for helping them so much; all I had really done was to listen, and say 'yes' and 'no' and make the usual noises of approval. Most people in that state of mind find it very difficult to talk to those near and dear to them.

I was appointed Director of the North Devon branch after a year, and found it to be a most challenging and rewarding post. I became involved, along with a team of leaders, as they are known, in preparing men and women to become volunteers to work in the branch. We trained about one hundred such people who came from all walks of life and from all denominations, or none at all. They were a wonderful group of people who became my very close friends, because, as Director, I had to know each one intimately — their history and their ability to listen to disturbed people, as well as sharing with them in their contacts with clients.

Many of the people who came to us needed practical help, and this we were able to provide by referral to professionals, such as psychiatrists, lawyers, housing authorities and others. Some of them needed help which we ourselves were able to give in the way of long-term friendship, and in cases of homelessness, some of us gave them shelter in our homes.

It was in this latter type of befriending that Dorothy and I were able to be of help. Many of these people, especially the young, were on drugs of various kinds, so I took them to our home where I found that I could help some of them to come off this evil addiction through hypnotic suggestion. It often meant that I would have to be with them for many hours, especially at night, when they were suffering from what is known as 'cold turkey' — that is, while they were going through their withdrawal symptons. The joy of seeing a beautiful young life being liberated from the clutches of the Devil, and restored to a normal life, is beyond description. I believe that all addictions are forms of possession.

At the end of the first three years at Bradford, I found that I had neglected to keep a proper balance between work and play. I had become so involved in my work, interesting and fascinating as it was, that my family had been neglected. So in addition to spending more time with them, I went back to my old hobby of music, but not making music as much as listening to it. Here Dorothy was able to share with me because she too loved good music. To help us in this I bought a really good tape recorder and joined a tape club which published some first class recordings of classical music. This we enjoyed late in the evenings when the children were in bed. The second reason for purchasing such a machine was to be able to record some of our services in church. These were later played back to elderly or infirm people who were unable to get to church. In the comfort of their own homes, they very much enjoyed being able to hear again something that had been very much a part of their lives in years gone by. This machine became most useful in those small churches when an organist was unable to be present. I recorded the singing of hymns by good choirs, and when the recorder was placed in the chancel it was just as if a choir was really present. Up to that time I had played the organ myself in the absence of the regular organist, but this meant bobbing up and down from my stall to the organ seat, which was very distracting for all. Another use for the recorder was at weddings. I have always given the newly married couple a recording of their marriage service, but with their promise that they would together listen to that recording on each anniversary, and renew their promises as they heard themselves doing on their wedding day.

When I went to Bradford and Thornbury, I continued to keep my contact with the mental hospitals, and at the same time seeking to create in Christian general practitioners, an interest in the part that the spiritual dimension of man has to play in their therapeutic work. I have always had a very sympathetic and positive response from doctors to such suggestions when presented in this way — a way that does not give the impression that here is a kind of magical formula that supersedes anything the medical profession can provide.

During the first centuries of Christianity, the Church was God's healing agent, the channel through which He brought healing and wholeness to sick people. It was in such places as monasteries that our hospitals had their birth, but after the fourth century the Church became popular and prosperous, and little by little the Pentecostal power that God had bestowed upon her began to weaken and wane. By the Middle Ages she was using the relics of saints and other weird methods to heal the sick. It was from that time that medical science began to make great progress, and so grow into that wonderful profession we know today. But all down the centuries there have been a few who have felt the need to emphasise the importance of keeping a balance between the material and the spiritual. I believe that the work of the doctor and the priest are complementary to one another, in that each is seeking to create conditions in a person's being, to enable healing and wholeness to take place.

A man may cut his hand, and if the conditions are right, that is, if the wound is sterile, the cut will heal without that person needing to resort to fervent prayer. We say that Nature will heal the wound, though some of us would say God will do the healing, because it is His will that it should be healed. But if some infection is allowed to become established in that wound, Nature or God cannot heal, because the conditions for healing do not exist; the laws that allow healing to take place have not been complied with. When a doctor or nurse seeks to create those conditions, and prevent further deterioration by administering antibiotics and the like, then healing proceeds again. The fact is, that whether it is positive thinking, the physician with his drugs, the surgeon with his scalpel or the priest seeking forgiveness of sins, they are all endeavouring to create the state in a person's being that is conducive to healing and wholeness. There are many conditions which prevent the healing of body, mind and spirit. Contrary to the thinking of many people, we are not made up of individual parts, like a machine, so that each can be treated separately and independently of the others. We are a whole being, with body, mind and spirit acting and reacting upon each other.

A lady called Alice was once referred to me with a terrible skin condition that had troubled her for seven years. She had been treated by doctors and dermatologists without any success. I saw her regularly each week, and we talked about her past life. Although Alice had been brought up a Christian, prayer at that time was not very meaningful to her. During our conversations I learnt that she and her brother had been orphaned when she was five years old, and had been brought up by a distant relative. They had no other relatives, so were thrown very close together; and when her brother married in his early twenties, she felt very much alone. But worse was to come: her sister-in-law left her brother not long after the marriage, which created a terrible hatred in Alice's heart against this woman whom she felt had hurt her dear brother so much. Her hatred was so intense that when she talked about it, her features became horribly distorted.

At each visit I talked to her about the healing love of Christ, and one day when I thought she was ready for it, I told her that her only hope of healing lay in a reconciliation with her sister-in-law. I went on to say that she should write to her and apologise for the terrible things she had said about her, and suggest they become friends again. Her reaction was immediate, leaving me in no doubt about the intensity of her hatred: 'What,' she said, 'love that so-and-so. Never.' I knew then that I still had a long way to go before there could be any kind of healing.

After many weeks of talking together about Christian principles and values, she opened the door to me one day and I realised that something wonderful had happened: her face was radiant. She said, 'You have been coming to see me for a long time, and I have learnt so much about the healing power of Christ. I have written to my sister-in-law, asking if she will forgive me all the awful things I have said about her and if we might be friends again.' Without any prompting from me, she went down on her knees and poured it all out to the Lord. I laid my hands upon her head in healing prayer, knowing instinctively that because she was healed spiritually, so she would be healed physically. Within a week there were signs of an improvement in her condition, and this continued until there was no sign of that horrible skin eruption. But that was not all — not only had she been healed of her skin condition, she had become a radiant Christian; she was made whole.

I was wonderfully supported in my work in the Ministry of Healing by a very dear friend. I had first met Guy Sanderson during my time in Tiverton, when he was rector of Silverton, and even that short acquaintance left me in no doubt that here was a priest who was being mightily used by God. Later he became Bishop of Plymouth; at that time I was at Bradford, and so I came under his jurisdiction. We have been close friends since that time, and have worked together in that ministry of the Church which has been so sadly neglected by the powers that be. I owe so much to Guy for his support in those days when I was treading a lonely road in the Healing Ministry.

We both felt that a prayer group should be an integral part of every parish and along with the parish priests we helped to arrange several in many parts of the diocese. I was constantly amazed and encouraged by Guy's enthusiasm for this very important work. He would make the long journey to North Devon and to other parts of the diocese in order to take part in a prayer group, and often not arrive home in Plymouth until after midnight. Our own prayer group at Bradford was what I used to call the powerhouse of the parish. The faithful souls who attended that group week after week made a much bigger contribution to the parish and its people, and even to the world beyond than they will ever realise. Not only did we uphold in prayer the needs of the sick and those who had problems, but every decision to be made by the parochial church council was first laid before the prayer group, seeking God's will for that particular project. We prayed, too, for guidance for the young people seeking confirmation, couples preparing for marriage and parents preparing for the baptism of their children.

Our years at Bradford seemed to pass so quickly. Our grandchildren, who by this time were getting more numerous, often came to stay with us, and share with the foster children in their fun and games. An event that gave Dorothy and me a great deal of joy was the marriage of our son Bill to June, who literally married 'the boy next door': June's parents had a small farm adjoining the rectory. Bishop Guy officiated at their wedding, where most of the guests seemed to be children and young people. The reception was held in the old tithe barn, where many such events had taken place down the years.

We had come to know the people of those little parishes as dear friends, sharing with them in their joys and sorrows and their work and play for nine years, when the bishop suggested that I should be thinking of accepting a greater responsibility and said, 'Would you like to go to Hartland?' My home parish was the last place had I expected to be offered, and when I explained to him that I had been born and brought up there, he said, 'That is all the more reason why you should go there; you know that parish and its people well.' My immediate reaction was, how wonderful to be going home to minister among my kith and kin — to stand at that altar, in that pulpit and to follow in the footsteps of the man to whom I owed so much, was almost overwhelming, but I put all those sentiments aside, and determined not to allow them to influence my ultimate decision in any way.

Dorothy and I talked and talked; we prayed that God would make His will known to us. Then, as if a message from Heaven, the words of Jesus stuck in my mind: 'A prophet is not without honour, save in his own country and house.' At first I tried to dismiss these words as not being applicable to me, and I obviously could not visit Hartland and ask my friends what they thought about it. So little by little I came to the sad conclusion that I must decline the bishop's offer. I felt it would be unfair to those dear people if I failed in my ministry to them because of familiarity. It would have been so hard if I had to make an unpopular decision and lost their confidence because I had gone to school with some of them, who knew me so well. So after many weeks of heart-searchings, I wrote to the bishop declining his invitation and giving my reasons.

I determined not to let that episode disturb my work in the parishes, so we settled down to the old way of life. But it was not to be for long; just two months later the bishop wrote again, inviting me to consider the living of North Molton and Twitchen. These parishes are on Exmoor, and I knew nothing of them; they were a part of the diocese I had never visited. Little did we think as we drove into North Molton village on our tour of inspection that it would become home to us in the deepest sense of the word.

We realised at once that here was tremendous scope for our initiative, with a population about three times as great as our present combined parishes, and the possibility of an even greater increase, with two housing estates being built. We were much impressed by the lovely parish church in North Molton, which, although it had been rather neglected, had wonderful potential. The church at Twitchen, tucked away in a fold in the hills of Exmoor, and serving that small community, was a most attractive little building, beautifully maintained. The black spot of our visit that day was the vicarage, built about 1802 and containing five bedrooms with a small cottage adjoining — the whole being in a very bad state of repair.

Again we got down to prayer and discussion, often lasting into the small hours of the night. Was it God's will that we should go to North Molton? Gradually we became convinced that we should go, even though there was so much which, from a material point of view, seemed to say, 'Why not stay where you are; you have a lovely home and garden, and so many friends.' To add to that argument was the question of whether or not we could cope with our four foster children in a more restricted environment, after the freedom of our garden and fields.

As the days and weeks passed, we felt more and more sure that God was calling us to North Molton. I was fifty-five years of age at that time, and knew that it would almost certainly be my last appointment before retirement. Another fact that influenced my decision was a very real desire to use my interest in the Ministry of Healing more fully, by having the opportunity for contact with doctors and hospitals, because I firmly believed that this ministry lay in complete co-operation with all aspects of healing. So it was that I wrote to the bishop accepting his invitation to become vicar of North Molton with Twitchen, with the proviso that the house would be put into a reasonable state of repair.

It was not until I had occasion to write to the patron of that Living that I realised I would be meeting up with someone I had known all my life, and who, like myself, was very much a part of Hartland — Lady Stucley. She was my patron, having inherited the patronage from her father, Lord Poltimore, and was also the wife of Sir Dennis Stucley. He, in turn, had inherited the Abbey at Hartland that had been so much a part of my young life, where they lived for the greater part of the year. So after all those years I had come full circle, as it were, in my contact with friends of former days — Sir Dennis's family having come to the Abbey some ten years before mine arrived in Hartland in 1550.

There was a great deal that needed to be done to the vicarage, which would take about nine months to complete, so it was decided that we should live in a little cottage further down in the village during that time. We were not enthusiastic about this idea at first, because the house was so small for our large family, and most of our furniture would have to be put into store for those months; then there would be the upheaval of moving again. We found that the cottage was called Rose Cottage — which we liked — but even more satisfying was the fact that it was in the middle of the village, right among the people I hoped to serve, so that I would get to know them quickly. We spent many hours with the architect, planning the alterations in the vicarage, and Dorothy enjoyed choosing the colour schemes; but all the while, at the back of our minds, there was the awful thought that soon we should have to say farewell to so many dear friends at Bradford and Thornbury.

It is not often that a priest in the Anglican Church had the opportunity to welcome his successor before leaving a parish; there is generally a lapse of many months before he is appointed. The parochial church council of Thornbury was the patron for that particular appointment and I was asked to join them in making their decision. Two men were duly interviewed, the first of which was asked by a member of the council if he was prepared to co-operate with the Methodist Church as I had done during my time in the parish, His reply was a very firm 'No', and I knew at once that he would not become the vicar of Thornbury. We had built up a very happy relationship with our friends at the Methodist Church, worshipping in each other's buildings at regular intervals — something that had never been done before, and the council rightly felt that they wished it to continue. The second man was known to me, having been a lay reader before ordination, and had served his Title in the parish of Holsworthy. We all felt sure that he would continue in the tradition to which the parishes had been accustomed. It was a great relief to know that the pattern of one's work would be continued by a man in whom one had complete trust.

At last the unhappy day dawned when I should take my last services at my two little churches, but I had not anticipated the trauma that would accompany them. The first was at Bradford where everything seemed to go wrong: my concentration went to pieces, I forgot parts of the service and announced the wrong hymns. Then came the presentation of lovely parting gifts by the churchwardens to Dorothy and myself, with the love of those wonderful people being manifested in their tears.

At Thornbury later that morning, the repercussions were even worse. When my faithful wardens, Jim and Tom, walked up the aisle to present the parishioners' parting gifts, neither of them could utter a word — their voices had gone completely. I could see Jim trying to say something, but no words came. To save them further embarrassment I started to express my thanks and say farewell, when without any warning, my voice ceased to function also. We three stood in the middle of the church full of people, none of us able to speak; this we all found most disconcerting, to say the least. The organist came to our rescue by starting to play the next hymn, after which my voice had returned and I was able to bow out gracefully and thankfully. That night Dorothy and I decided we could never go through the agony of another such farewell, and that the next parish must be our last.

The next morning the vans were at our door to take some of our furniture to the little cottage in North Molton and the remainder to be put in store until the vicarage had been repaired. After they had gone, Dorothy and I walked quietly through that lovely house, now so empty, reliving with thankfulness the years we had been privileged to be there. We thanked God for all the little ones He had loaned us during those years, and who had given us so much joy; the teenagers who had come with their problems and difficulties, and who, through his help, were now happily settled in their homes. Then in prayer together, we commended all the dear people of those parishes to God's care and with a final backward glance at our lovely home, we set off into the unknown, but with the absolute assurance that we would be given the same spiritual guidance and help we had enjoyed throughout our ministry.

18

My Call to Exmoor

We found Rose Cottage to be rather smaller than we had anticipated, especially with the four children. We soon settled in, much to the surprise of the parishioners who had not been used to being on such intimate terms with the vicar and his family and having him live in their midst rather than in the seclusion of the vicarage. The children, too, were a source of great delight — my predecessor was the incumbent for thirty-four years and had no family.

My Institution was conducted by my beloved Bishop Wilfred Westall who had been such a support to me before my ordination. The Induction was performed by Archdeacon Arthur Ward, my colleague in the Samaritans. I was presented to the bishop by my patron, Lady Stucley, so I felt very much among friends, which made it an especially happy occasion; it was, too, for the parishioners, because a great number of them had never before witnessed such an event. The church was full to capacity, and after the little churches of Bradford and Thornbury, All Saints at North Molton seemed huge in comparison. It was such a joy to have some of my friends from the previous parishes supporting me by their presence and prayers, including Les, my warden for the whole of my time at Bradford; also Hugh Manning, who had been a tower of strength to me during the stewardship campaign; both their lives had been greatly touched by the campaign.

The Benefice of All Saints, North Molton, was united with that of St Peter, Twitchen, so that only one service of institution was necessary, though, of course, the wardens and congregation of the latter church were present at that service. The wardens at North Molton were Henry Ayre and John Govier, while at Twitchen I had Mrs Maria Hill and Harry Thorne. They proved to be such faithful friends and staunch supporters of their church that most of them were still in office when I left those parishes eleven years later.

My predecessor, the Reverend Walter Prew, had decided to spend his retirement in the parish and had moved to a little cottage in the village a year before I arrived. I was a little troubled about this at first, because the presence of a previous incumbent has been known to cause trouble, and he had been the vicar there for more than thirty years. But there was no such problems with Walter Prew, who came to see me on the day after our arrival in the village and gave me the absolute assurance that he would do all he could to make my ministry a happy one. And he did just that.

I shall never forget the wonderful welcome that was given to Dorothy and myself when we were invited to meet the parochial church council at the home of Maurice and Joan Whinney, two days after the institution. It was a grand opportunity to get to know those people with whom I was to work so closely in the years ahead. I found them to be a quite different type of people from those dear friends in Bradford and Thornbury. It was interesting to notice the different attitude to life taken by the farmers, for instance. The environment in which people are born and brought up has a lasting effect upon their spirituality. I found the farmers of Exmoor to be much more aware of the existence of God, and the reality of His love and power in their lives than was the case with their contemporaries in the more rewarding farming areas in the other parts of the country. It seems to be a case of the easier life becomes, the less thought is given to the source of material things. For many years the farmers of

Exmoor had scraped a living out of very reluctant and often harsh land, and the generation with which I was involved had been brought up under those conditions — always grateful for the little they had. But during my years on Exmoor I saw a change take place. Largely because of the subsidies and grants given by the government, the farmers of Exmoor became more prosperous. One saw so many domestic luxuries and accessories appearing in their homes; things that would have been undreamed of a few years earlier. Outside on the farms, too, the most modern aids were to be seen being used, the cost of which must have been colossal.

Along with that change one noticed another and more sinister one — mainly in the next generation of farmers. This was a lessening of interest in things spiritual, and of the need to come to the source of all supply. Harvest Festivals were still well patronised, but there seemed to be an underlying reluctance on the part of many to accept the fact that God alone supplies our every need. Yet, in spite of that, it was among the farming community that I felt there was the deepest awareness of God. The majority of the people who came to live in the housing estates which were built during my years at North Molton, most of whom worked in the factories at South Molton, seemingly had no need of the Church and the deeper realities of life. Another problem I found with this latter type of people was their lack of interest, not only in the Church, but in the general life of the village. Many of them had come from cities and large towns and they found it difficult to become integrated into the social life of the community. This presented a real challenge to me as the parish priest. I felt that because my work was to bring people to Christ, it had to begin where those people were and in the situation in which they found themselves. An important part of that work was the uniting of those newcomers with the original residents of the village.

My wardens, Henry and Jack, were a constant source of support to me during those weeks following my institution. I remember how we spent three evenings going through the voters list for the parishes; this was in order to give me details of each person, their background, their allegiances to our own or other churches, and those to whom they were related in the parishes. This latter point is of great importance when coming into a comparatively small community; it saves much embarrassment in the early months of one's ministry in that parish.

The work of restoration on the vicarage went ahead slowly — much too slowly for Dorothy and me, who wished to get safely installed there before the onset of winter. But before that could take place, another problem loomed up on the horizon. During my time at Bradford I had had two attacks of renal colic necessitating on one occasion I painfully remember, a forty-mile bumpy journey to Plymouth hospital at 2 am. It was discovered then that I also had gallstones, although these had up to that time not made themselves known to me. So that they should not have the opportunity to do so, I decided after consultation with my doctor to have them removed as soon as possible. In two days I found myself in hospital at Bideford — back among the doctors and staff I knew so well — awaiting the final pre-med jab before going into the operating theatre.

I shall never forget the look of surprise on the face of Sister Mary when she came to give me that injection, and I asked her to wait just a moment while I said 'Grace'. 'Grace!' she said, 'You're not going to have anything to eat, you are going for surgery.' I then asked her to be patient just for a moment while I explained what I meant by Grace. I knew she was a Christian who would be sympathetic to what I had to say. I told her that the prayer I intended to use was, 'Bless, O Lord, this surgery to your healing use and myself in your service.' I tried to show her that although Dr H would operate, he would not heal my body — he would merely remove the offending organ and so create the conditions for God to do His work of healing. The physician administers drugs, but these do not heal; they, too, create the conditions for healing to take place. Together we said our prayer; our 'Grace' that God would take the surgeon's mind and think through it; that He would take his hand and use the instruments as a channel or means towards my healing. Then committing myself to God's care, she gave me the final jab, and I was 'away'. I have often been amazed at the power of the right word at the right time, and so it was with Sister Mary. She was so impressed that she has taught many people since that day to think along those lines, and I know with what wonderful results.

After three weeks of convalescence I was back at work again, by which time our vicarage was ready for occupation. So again we moved house, almost exactly five months after coming to the parishes. All this put a heavy burden upon Dorothy, but this was lessened to some extent by the fact that she had more room to cope with the children and

I would again have my study and room in which to interview parishioners, as well as those who came to seek healing.

North Molton nestles in the foothills of Exmoor facing south, three miles north-east of the market town of South Molton. On the north side of the parish there are the remains of Bronze Age settlements dating back to 1900–500 BC. These are on the highest parts of the parish, rising to 1600 feet above sea level. There are several groups of burial places or barrows, as they are called, including eight at one spot. In one of these was found what is known as the North Molton Necklace; this was found in 1889 and is now in the Exeter Museum.

In 700 AD, after the Saxon conquest, North Molton was made a key settlement by the king, its function to overawe the remnants of the old Celtic race who had been dispossessed of their lands. There are several farms on the west side of the parish which still retain their Celtic names, like Walscott. At the time of the Domesday Survey in 1086 North Molton was one of the most valuable royal manors in Devon, paying £45 per annum. This had been granted by Edward the Confessor to his wife for her support. At that time there were forty-four villeins — this indicates the probable number of separate holdings, each representing a family. There were fifty bordars, who worked the lord's land and had a small-holding of their own, and eleven serfs — probably individuals, not families, who had no rights whatever.

Between 1100 and 1200 the parish of Twitchen was separated from that of North Molton. The church at Twitchen has a Norman font, which indicates that there must have been a church to house it at that time. In 1209 the manor and church was presented by King John to Roger La Zouche, and sixty years later he granted the lord of the manor the right to hold a weekly market and annual fair — the latter to be held on All Saints day, the patronal festival.

At the taxation of Pope Nicholas IV in 1288 the parish was assessed to pay £33. 6. 8d, one of the largest amounts in the county, which shows that there must have been a thriving settlement there. The parish had four corn mills and one fulling mill by 1314, the latter processing locally woven cloth made from the wool of the large flocks of sheep run in the parish and, in the summer, in the Exmoor forest. It is said that there are more sheep per acre in North Molton today than anywhere else in the world, including New Zealand.

By 1361 a great deal of the land in the

parish was untilled because of the ravages of the Black Death some years previously, which had carried off large numbers of the population including the vicar. Two corn mills had ceased to work, and much arable land had been converted to 'sheep walks'. The first mention of the copper mines was made in 1346 when Nicholas de Wellifors was made the keeper of the king's copper mines, but they are believed to have been worked first by the Romans. The present church was built in the early part of the fifteenth century, from stone dug in the parish, on the site of the original Norman church. It was at this time that the village was named as a borough — a self-governing community with a portreeve as its head and with other officers such as the scavenger, the dog catcher, the keeper of the peace and the ale tasters. The last portreeve was elected as late as 1935.

In 1662 the vicar, John Hill, was ejected from the living for not signing the Act of Uniformity. In that year, according to a census by Bishop Compton, there were seven hundred and fifty Anglicans, eighteen Protestant Dissenters and no Roman Catholics living in the parish. A school was begun in 1713, and John Wesley came to stay in the village in 1757. A Sunday school was started in 1821 for one hundred and fifty children, where they were also taught to read and write. By 1863 the numbers had been reduced to one hundred and three, but when Lord Poltimore, the lord of the manor, gave a tea party for the scholars in that year two hundred and fifty children turned up! At the Crimean War celebration in 1856, eight hundred people sat down to a meal in the village square. The longest recorded incumbency of a vicar of North Molton was fifty-eight years by John Grade.

During the latter part of the nineteenth century the remaining five copper and iron mines were closed because the pumps of that date could not cope with the amount of water which flowed into them. In 1971 one of the pits was pumped dry with a view to reopening it. The headmaster of the council school, Peter Bassett, and myself expressed a desire to go down in a bucket to look at those old workings.

I would not have missed that experience for anything. We bumped our way down through that hole in the ground, some six feet square, with boulders protruding on all sides, against which our bucket on the end of a wire rope constantly collided, almost tipping us out. On reaching the bottom, after dropping one hundred and sixty feet, a marvellous sight met our eyes: because of the copper pyrites, in the light of our small torches the walls of the mine shone like gold, literally gold — fool's gold as it is called. There, too, were the seams of iron ore marked with the pick marks of the men who had laboured there hundreds of years before. It was an eerie sensation walking through those tunnels, with the sound of rushing water reverberating from the old workings at even deeper levels. Sometimes we were in passageways some six feet in height; then after crawling through an opening no more than three feet high, we found ourselves in the most wonderful cavernous type of place, with even more examples of fool's gold lining the walls. My regret is that I did not take a flash camera with me — the beauty had to be seen to be believed. We spent almost an hour in that mine which had been filled with water for a hundred years, marvelling at the courage and tenacity of the men who had worked there in such terrible conditions — some of them possibly having spent all their working lives down there. Every piece of ore had to be carried in buckets through those small openings to the foot of the shaft where it was transported on a narrow gauge railway to the mainline station at South Molton.

Twitchen is a beautiful little hamlet, higher up on the moor than North Molton, but like its bigger neighbour, nestling in a fold in the hills. Here as in most such isolated communities, there is a wonderful sense of comradeship. Everyone works happily with everyone else, whether it is in the skittle team, the Womens' Institute or the Church — barriers seem to be non-existent.

Exmoor is a very beautiful area in which to live — even in winter when work on the farms is not at all easy, as J. H. Turner has made clear in the following lines

The poets of these present days
Sing sweetly sentimental lays,
Of rippling streams and purple heather;
They seldom write of winter weather.
What do these men, of nature, know
Of hurricanes that rage and blow
The slates and sheets of galvanize
Soaring like seagulls through the skies,
Torn from our house and shed,
While warm and snug, they lie, them-
    selves abed?
They have no bullocks to be fed
Nor rise to find their best cow dead
At foggy morn,
No lambs reluctant to be born
By aid of flickering lantern-light,
In the dead hours of wintry night;
They are not troubled in their sleep

With dreams about their helpless sheep
Buried in the driven snow.
Naught do they know
Of all the ills
Besetting stock upon the hills;
Parturient septicaemia;
Of deadly parasites and germs
Of liver fluke and worms,
Of hypomagnesaemia.

But conditions are not always like that. When the summer sun drenches the heather and bracken, and the warm breezes waft across those rolling hills, Exmoor is like a little corner of heaven. The call of a lamb to its mother, echoing across the valleys from one hillside to another; the plaintive cry of a buzzard, wheeling high above on a thermal current, and the gurgle of a moorland stream hurrying on its way to the sea — all these are sounds deeply implanted in my memory, for which I am grateful.

The red deer, too, were very much a part of the lovely Exmoor scene. Often, as I drove across the moor on a quiet summer morning, a herd of twenty or thirty would trot down a lane in front of me. I well remember one incident, just as the dawn was breaking and I was driving to an early service down a very narrow lane with high banks on either side, a huge stag suddenly appeared spreadeagled in the air above the bonnet of the car. It had been jumping from one bank to the other, and I expect it was as surprised as I was to meet in such circumstances.

During my years at Exmoor I saw more and more people coming for their holidays each year. On that vast expanse of land one can walk or sunbathe or swim in the streams, and hardly ever see another human being in the course of a day. Many people prefer this wonderful solitude to the overcrowded beaches and the dangers of some bathing areas. My favourite spot, to which Dorothy and I often went, was North Molton Common. From there we could look out over the whole of Bideford Bay, with Lundy Island in the far distance, and the light at Hartland Point flashing its warning signal to shipping at night. I knew, too, that beyond the high ground on the horizon lay that parish of which I felt so much a part, and to whose people I seemed to be so close.

19

New Horizons

Lovely as Exmoor is, there was work to be done in North Molton and Twitchen. We quickly settled into our reconditioned vicarage which we found to be very cosy and warm, even in an Exmoor winter, but I soon discovered that there was a great deal to be done to the church building at North Molton, as well as building up the spiritual Church in the parish. I well remember walking up the churchyard path one morning during a severe gale — the like of which so often sweeps across the moor, when I saw one of the pinnacles on the church tower swaying in the wind. I thought at first that my eyes were deceiving me, but no, with each strong gust the pinnacle swayed a little. Along with the churchwardens I climbed to the top of the one hundred and ten foot tower, where I found my suspicions confirmed. There was no cement on the base of the pinnacle to hold it in position; its sheer weight alone prevented it from crashing to the ground. We quickly made arrangements to have it, and the other three pinnacles, taken down — an operation which proved to be far from easy. In this we were greatly helped by the experience of the Priest brothers, who did a wonderful job under dangerous conditions.

All this cost a lot of money, and our bank balance was at a very low level. This fact proved to be a blessing in disguise, because it gave me the opportunity to get down to some teaching on the art of giving. The parochial church council and I spent many hours working out a plan, whereby every Church person in the parish was given information and guidance on how they should see themselves as stewards of God's gifts. We tried to show them that nothing they possessed was really theirs, but that all they had was loaned to them for a few years and left behind.

I found the church council at North Molton to be much more alert to its responsibilities than those in other parishes. Here I was to benefit from my experiences at Bradford and Thornbury when I formed a prayer group. This was a very successful venture again, and we met at regular intervals to hold our plan, and the people to whom it would apply, up to God and seek His will. There were some very dedicated people in that group to whom this manner of prayer was not new, so we made great strides quickly. This continued all through my years in that parish, and was indeed a very real 'powerhouse'. The result of this was a new surge of spirituality throughout the parish. The most unexpected people came to offer themselves and their time and talents to God, just as the people of Bradford had done, even though the methods used were different. Our income at North Molton went up from £300 per year to £1400 and again, as in my previous parish, there was a real improvement in the number of regular worshippers. But in this case the improvement in attendance was seen in young couples with their children.

I was fortunate in this because many of the new houses, as they were built, were occupied by young people and it was on these that I concentrated on first coming into the parish. There had been no Sunday school for some years, so with this potential of children we got busy on that important function of the work of the Church. There were two faithful Sunday school teachers of years gone by, who at once offered their services again, even though they were by that time well advanced in years. Miss Ethel Smith and Mrs William Tucker helped so much to prepare the way for younger teachers to come forward. Teacher Ethel, as she was affectionately known, had been a teacher at the council school. She seemed to have taught the majority of the people of North Molton, and was loved and respected by all.

A turning point in the worshipping life of the parish church was the introduction of a family service each month. Although all age groups were catered for at this service, it was especially planned with the young in mind. A choir of twenty-five young people under the age of sixteen years was formed, for whom we bought robes. Here I would pay tribute to Miss Caroline Durston-Smith, a great musician who helped me wonderfully. The children loved her and knew her well because she taught at the primary school.

The children took an active part in the services by reading the scriptures, and by singing special hymns and songs, all under Caroline's guidance. The whole atmosphere of worship seemed to change from that time; there was a joy I had not noticed before. Tiny tots would wander up the aisle and hold out their arms to be picked up as I talked to the congregation. Here I would like to say how grateful I was to the older members of that worshipping community for their tolerance and patience with the young. There was, inevitably, noise and disturbance from time to time, but not once did I have a complaint. I thought that this was so wonderful, especially when I remembered that small children had hardly ever been seen in that church before.

The next step was to introduce those young people to a service of Holy Communion. The experimental services were just being introduced in some churches at that time, so we chose Series Three as being the most suitable for family worship. The children took to it easily and happily, though there was some misgiving on the part of a few older people at the use of the words 'You' and 'Your', instead of 'Thee' and 'thine'.

Someone has written an amusing poem about this called 'An Old Woman's Lament':

They've brought you up to date, Lord,
 up at All Saints,
They've pensioned off the organ, and
 they're praising with guitars.
They've done it for the young ones, we
 want to bring them in,
But I do wish they could worship
 without making such a din,
For I'm growing rather deaf, Lord, and
 when there's all that noise,
It gets so very hard, Lord, to hear your
 loving voice.
They've written brand new hymns, Lord,
 with tunes that I don't know,

So I hardly ever sing now, though I did
 love singing so.
They're very go ahead, Lord, they're
 doing Series Three,
But the words are not so beautiful as the
 others used to be.
They've modernised the Bible, and the
 Lord's Prayer and the Creed,
When the old ones were so perfect that
 they filled my every need.
My mind's not quite so agile as it was
 some years ago,
And I miss the age-old beauty of the
 words I used to know.
It's very clear to me, Lord, I've
 overstayed my time,
I don't take to change so kindly as I did
 when in my prime.
But it can't be very long before I'm
 called above,
And I know I'll find you there, Lord, and
 glory in your love.
So till then I'll stick it here, though it's
 not the same for me,
But while others call you 'You' Lord, do
 you mind if I say 'Thee'?

It did not take those older people long to accept the new language, and this I found to be rather wonderful, because country folk generally find it harder to accept change than do their town and city cousins.

After our first years at North Molton we decided to take a holiday, never having been away from our home for a break since ordination. Dorothy had become very involved with her foster children and teenagers in trouble, as well as the occasional drug addict and homeless person that came our way, and she badly needed to get away from it all. I, too, looked forward to a week or two of complete relaxation. The pressures of moving into a new parish, with all the inevitable problems that arose, along with my work with the Samaritans, plus the travelling involved in the Ministry of Healing, all added up to a longing to be alone with Dorothy.

We arranged to have two weeks on one of the canals, where we felt we would have a free and easy holiday away from people. Our cruise on the Grand Union and Oxford Canals proved to be just the kind of break we both needed. Our little boat was beautifully furnished and very comfortable; we had the freedom to travel as little or as much as we wanted, and to tie up for the night where and when we wished — this, plus glorious weather, combined to make our first holiday one we shall never forget.

Back in the parishes, feeling refreshed and

ready to tackle whatever came along, we soon settled back into our normal routine. But this was not to be for long. The bishop invited me to take charge of an additional parish a little higher up on the moor, called Molland. The incumbent of that parish was Bert Venton — an old friend from my farming days. He, too, had been a lay reader at the same time as myself, and had gone to King's two years before me. He had now decided to retire and live in the village where he had been vicar.

It had been such a joy when I came to North Molton to find Bert in the Deanery, and be able to renew our friendship. We had a great deal in common, so I was sure that we would have no problems about him living in the parish for his retirement, and so it proved to be. In fact, I was often very grateful that he was there to stand in for me, when snow and ice prevented me from getting across the moor to officiate at some services in the winter months. Some of the hills in that area have gradients of one in four, and often I have set out for a service at one of the parishes at a higher level, become stranded and been forced to abandon the car.

Molland is a tiny parish of some three hundred inhabitants about seven miles from North Molton. The church is of unspoilt sixteenth-century architecture, with a three-decker pulpit and horse-box pews; whenever one invited the congregation to pray, the church suddenly appeared to become empty, as everyone disappeared from view behind those high pews.

Taking on an extra parish meant that there had to be some rearrangement of the Sunday services, but this proved not to be difficult when the three church councils met together and worked out a plan, as well as finding ways of sharing their priest in an economical way. I received wholehearted support from the people of Molland, who, although they were obviously disappointed that they could no longer have a priest of their own as they had done since 1660, accepted the fact that financial circumstances and manpower shortage made it inevitable.

In Molland, as in most other parishes, there was a nucleus of faithful souls who were always ready to do all in their power to forward the work of Christ. My warden, Ron Crook, then a postman, was a tower of strength to me, as was his wife, Betty, who had played the organ in that church for over fifty years. The ringers, too, were always an inspiration to me by their faithfulness in ringing the bells at every evening service. Captain John Pugsley had led his team to win many trophies at ringing competitions all over North Devon. The singing of that little congregation, too, was such a joy, and I have often gone home with the hymns ringing in my ears. The prayer group we formed at Molland was the smallest I have known, but powerful none the less. They were a dynamic little group who really enjoyed their work and worshipping life. I am sure that any priest would have been proud to work with them.

One of the two doctors' practices at South Molton had held a surgery twice weekly at a house in North Molton for many years, but after our first year in the parish this arrangement was discontinued. The doctors found it impossible to find another house in North Devon with two rooms suitable for their purpose, so Dorothy and I offered to accommodate them. It gave me an opportunity to get to know the people who were sick, and also to work more closely with the doctors, who were great Christians.

I had always taught my people to call for me when they had occasion to call a doctor, and quite often the result was that the doctor and I met on the doorstep. He would do what he felt necessary, then I would seek to help the patient in the way I thought to be right — at the same time impressing upon him or her that the doctor and I were, in reality, doing the same work — each seeking in his own field to contribute to that state of wholeness which God desires. The co-operation with my medical friends did much to strengthen my conviction that the Ministry of Healing was that aspect of the whole ministry to which God had called me.

We formed a discussion group composed of doctors and clergy where we shared one another's experiences and thoughts on the work of healing. We came to see it as the whole redemptive work of Christ: the practical way in which man in his unwholeness reaches out to that abundant life which Christ has promised, which means wholeness of body, mind and spirit. This, we felt, was the good news that Christ came to give to man — eternal life He called it — but that word eternal is often misunderstood. He meant it to have a qualitative basis rather than a quantitive one, embracing all those qualities of love and joy, peace and wisdom, wholeness and goodness. His will is that these should be expressed completely in the lives of men and women.

This was the work that Christ Himself did, and this is what He commanded His apostles to do during His earthly life: 'Preach the Gospel and heal the sick.' It was with that same command that He sent His Church into the world: 'As my father hath sent me, even so send I you.' Christ healed all who came to him; He never refused to heal and He never suggested to anyone that it might be God's will for sickness to continue, or that it was a good thing. In fact, He said it was completely contrary to the perfect will of God; He referred to 'this woman whom Satan hath bound these eighteen years'.

We agreed that there is still a deep-seated belief, albeit rarely expressed, that sickness and disease can sometimes be the direct will of God. But what alarmed us was our conclusion that this belief is often a very real barrier to wholeness. God is ever working in all Creation to express His wholeness and perfection. Somewhere along the line of our evolutionary process, God gave to man alone, as far as we know, the wonderful gift of free will, the power of choice. By the misuse of this gift, disharmony, disease and evil have come into His Creation. In this sense he has allowed sickness and disease, but it is His secondary will, as it were; He could not go back on His word and deny us that power of choice just because we have misused it.

Guy Sanderson and I continued to teach and be taught at the conferences we attended each year in various parts of the country; we were joined by Agnes Sandford, that great lady from the United States of America who had done so much to further this work in Christ's name, along with others of all denominations in this country who shared our thoughts. These gatherings of likeminded people helped me so much — both in the parishes and in my contact with people who came from outside.

During my third year at North Molton, a new Health Centre was built in South Molton, and I was privileged to be able to use a room there, in which to see people who had been referred to me. I well remember the first person I sought to help at that centre — a young man who suffered from claustrophobia. He was a lorry driver who had to give up his job because he felt so 'shut-in' in the cab of his lorry. He enjoyed a pint of beer, but always parked his car outside the pub in such a position that he could make a quick getaway when that awful feeling came over him. To drink his beer, he always had to stand at the door of the pub. I had seen this lad on two or three occasions, and used hypnotherapy to help him. At his next appointment I arranged for a doctor to be present; I always appreciated this, because it gave me the advantage of his professional knowledge in medical matters, especially with those conditions which were outside my ken. I suggested to the doctor that I thought the patient was ready for a practical application of post-hypnotic suggestion with regard to his claustrophobia.

The young man was put under hypnosis, and I suggested to him that when he awoke he would go into a pub on the other side of the town square which the Health Centre overlooked, and that he would feel very happy and relaxed in there, with no claustrophobic feelings whatever. The doctor and I watched him as he went out into the street at the end of his treatment. He stood on the pavement for a short while looking up and down as if unable to decide which way to go, then suddenly he started to cross the square and disappeared from our sight into the pub. I had already made an appointment to see him the next evening, and the doctor had agreed to be there also. The young man told us that when he got outside the Health Centre he felt a great urge to go into the pub opposite for a drink. Because he did not normally frequent that place, he hesitated for some time, but at last decided to go in. He told us that he had not felt so much at ease in a pub for a long time, and thought it must be something to do with the building, not realising that he was acting on a suggestion. From then on, I sought to apply this to his work of lorry driving, and very soon he was back at work with no sign of claustrophobia.

Back in the parishes life went on as usual, with all the joys and difficulties that are part of the work of a parish priest. During my second year we formed a youth club and a camera club, both of which were very successful and enjoyed to the full. I was also brought into other secular activities such as the Parish Council, School Managers, Parish Hall Committee and the South Molton District Council. On all these bodies I found opportunity to serve the parishes whose people I had promised to serve in Christ's name.

One of the most interesting church organisations in which I participated was a discussion group at North Molton. This was very well attended by all kinds of people and gave them the opportunity to ask many questions which had troubled them for so long. In my visiting I came to know and love my people in their home environment; because of my farming background I was able to speak the language of the farmers and so enter into a close relationship with them. I was often able to help them with their milking, for instance, when they were ill, and in other emergencies on the farm. Because I had been in their situation, I did not expect them to be in church at eight o'clock in the morning when they had fifty cows to milk, or were in the middle of lambing four hundred ewes. But on the other hand, I sometimes had to remind them — when they were consistently absent from church at other times, and made the excuse that they were too busy — that if there was a meet of the foxhounds or the staghounds in the village at 11 am, they would find the time to be there.

We had been so thrilled and refreshed by our canal holiday at the end of our first year in the parishes that we decided to repeat it. This time we took two friends with us on a bigger boat — a doctor friend and his wife, Harry and Eileen Durston-Smith, and we had a wonderful holiday together. This time we explored the Shropshire Canal starting at Stourport and travelling north to the River Trent, which we found to be most exciting.

In my work with the Samaritans, I sometimes became involved with young people who were addicted to drugs — many of whom had left their homes in other parts of the country, or had no home. Several of these unfortunate teenagers made their home with us, during which time I sought to help them overcome their problem through hypnotherapy, and help them to go on to lead a normal life. One beautiful girl had only just started her nursing training when she got involved with drugs. Another who lived with us for several years from time to time had had a terribly unhappy childhood and spent a considerable amount of time in prison for various offences, but always returned to 'Mum and Dad' each time she came out. We had a very bright young man come to stay with us, who had become addicted to LSD; he was in such a bad state that he attempted suicide. We found that most of these young people, and many others, responded to a loving and caring environment.

During our third year at North Molton, a note of sadness crept into our lives. My parents had made their home with my brother on the farm but they came to stay with us for several weeks each year. It was on one such occasion that my mother had a heart attack and died in her sleep. She was eighty-four years old, and had lived a full and happy life; no one could have had a more wonderful mother. We felt that her death called for thankfulness and joy, rather than mourning. She was laid to rest among her relatives and friends of the old days, in our home church where she had been so happy as a young wife and mum. The whole service was one of joy, with Easter hymns and the assurance that the mother whom we had known and loved was more alive than in the flesh. I felt this to be especially so when I was privileged to commit her to God's care at the grave. My father gradually deteriorated after her death, as is often the case when one is left alone after sixty years of married life. He passed to his rest three years later — again while staying with us.

During my third year in the parish, I was invited by the headmaster of the primary school to take the morning assembly. This was a wonderful opportunity for the children to see that the vicar was not only concerned with what they did in church on Sunday, but was also interested and involved with them as young people, every day of the week. As a result of this, the school became more and more involved in the worshipping life of the Church, as well as making use of the building at other times. Another development that gave me great joy at about the same time was the increased co-operation between our Anglican Church and the Methodist Church. We held monthly services alternately in each others buildings, and every three months we joined together for a service of Holy Communion. During my time at North Molton, three deaconesses served the Methodist Church and I found them to be most friendly and co-operative young ladies. The deaconesses and I used to meet once a month to discuss matters of mutual interest, and to pass on to one another information about parishioners who needed help in both Churches.

20

Experiences in Exorcism

Time seemed to go so quickly that three years had passed as if they had been months. It was then that I began to realise I was becoming involved in too many things. I had been Director of the Samaritans for five years and I felt the time had come for someone else to take over that responsibility. In fact, it was good for the branch that this should be so. I had seen that branch grow into a caring, efficient organisation, where empathy was the controlling factor, and which was trusted and respected by professionals and the public alike. I had had seven wonderful years with that group of people, each one of whom I am still proud to call my friend. So it was with sadness, yet with complete confidence, that I handed over my job to Chris Willis, who had been my right-hand man for some time.

This gave me more time to devote to the parishes, which, after all, were my prime concern, but also to develop my deep interest in the Ministry of Healing, which I saw as being basic to all my work as a priest. Guy continued to support me from his retirement in Somerset and we spent long hours in discussion over another aspect of that ministry that had always intrigued me — the question of possession and exorcism.

For some years I had had an open mind on the reality of a personal devil. In my ordinary pastoral ministry I sometimes came face to face with a situation that could not be explained away in ordinary human terms. Then there were those cases in the mental hospital which psychiatrists seemed unable to help. Guy and I decided to study the gospels afresh, to see what Jesus really intended His Church to do in this particular field of healing. When we looked again, for instance, at that terrible struggle between Jesus and Satan, or the 'prince of this world' as He called him, we came to the conclusion that here was no psychological encounter, but evil personified in reality. Jesus was the perfect psychologist but he never explained evil away in what may now be called psychological terms. He met it face to face and overcame it for what it was — the enemy of His Father's perfect will.

Christ's Church is concerned not only with the healing of the body, mind and spirit as such, but with that which often causes the sickness — the spiritual warfare against all forces of evil. As St Paul put it, 'Our fight is not against human foes, but against cosmic powers; against the authorities and potentates of this dark world; against the superhuman forces of evil in the heavens.' After much study and prayer, I decided that this was to be a part of my work in the Ministry of Healing. I immediately got down to the task of gaining as much experience as possible by working with a colleague in that field, where my first encounter with evil at an exorcism was very dramatic.

My friend had been asked to visit a man whom it was suspected had been influenced by evil, and suggested that I should go with him. On arriving at the house we were shown into a room where a man was sitting in a chair with a dog at his side. Almost immediately the man became very violent and abusive; his countenance became distorted, and he rose from his chair and rushed at my friend who calmly began to pray in Christ's name that he may be a channel for this sick man's healing, and that he himself may be surrounded by Christ's protecting power. By this time the man was in a terrible state of frenzy, and tried to grab my colleague by the throat, but for some reason which I did not understand until later, he failed to reach him. My friend then began to command the evil power that was controlling this man to come out of him in Christ's name. This he did in no uncertain terms. The man then collapsed on the floor, frothing at the mouth — a phenomenon that occurs at every exorcism, just as it did when our Lord cast out evil.

That was an absorbing experience for me and I was most impressed by the calmness that accompanied the whole thing, which gave me the assurance that a greater power than ours was in control. Nevertheless, from that day I often wondered how I would react if faced with a similar situation. I felt sure I was being called to this partucular aspect of my own ministry, so I sought to prepare myself for it by prayer and meditation. It was not long before I was called to see my bishop to talk about the whole question of exorcism. There had been two or three unfortunate incidents at that time in different parts of the country, where a great deal of damage had been done by people who did not know what they were doing and were not even able to diagnose possession, let alone exorcise correctly. My bishop, along with many others, decreed that no priest in his diocese should attempt an exorcism without having first referred the case to him. He then told me that he had appointed four priests, of whom I was to be one, to take charge of that aspect of the ministry in his diocese.

Within a few weeks of my appointment I had a call from a very worried lady whose husband had, for several years, been acting in a strange way from time to time. He would be quite normal for a few weeks then suddenly it was as if his whole personality became transformed into an aggressive, domineering and at times enraged character. He had sought psychiatric help without any results. His wife summed up the problem by saying that she had had fourteen years of married hell. I agreed to see the husband, so with a friend to drive, they set off on the seventy-mile journey to North Molton at nine o'clock in the evening, and arrived at my vicarage just before midnight. The man was by this time in a very disturbed state, and he rushed through the door shouting, 'Where is Fred Pennington? I want to get hold of him.' I was by this time quite prepared for anything he might do or say, having spent the previous two hours in prayer and meditation. Dorothy took the wife and friend into the kitchen and gave them coffee, while I began what was to be the first of many fascinating and dramatic cases in my ministry to the possessed.

While watching my collegue at work previously I had realised that the most important part of my exorcism was to make a correct diagnosis. I knew how subtle evil personified could be, and how it could cause a person to act and say things that were completely false. I knew, too, that when under hypnosis a person always answered truthfully to any question, so I decided to use that medium as my method of diagnosis. Having put the man into that state, I proceeded to question him until I was fully convinced that here was a genuine case of possession.

I felt I was being guided to do two things in this my first case of exorcism. First, to carry out that exorcism while the man was still under hypnosis, and in so doing to by-pass, as it were, his conscious mind, and simply be a channel for Christ in his work of destroying the evil power which was controlling this man. Secondly, to know myself to be surrounded by Christ's protecting power, so that I lost all sense of fear, and simply allowed Christ to take my lips and speak through them whatever words He desired. This is how I have acted in every exorcism since that day.

The manifestations of that first exorcism could not have been more dramatic if they had come from some novelist's pen. As I made the sign of the cross, while commanding evil to depart in Christ's name, the man suddenly opened his eyes. This is unknown in an ordinary session of hypnotherapy, but they had become blood red, and twice their normal size. They became fixed on me, and at the same time his lips seemed to twist into a leering sneer so that his teeth appeared as fangs. He then arose from his chair, still under hypnosis of course, and came towards me with his hands outstretched as if they were claws. As he slowly approached me, he began to speak in a voice that was totally unlike his own. He said, 'I am not coming out of him. I don't want to come out of him.' He repeated these words several times, getting closer and closer to me until his hands were almost touching my face. I stood quite still and continued to use the form of exorcism with which I had begun; suddenly and without any warning, he collapsed on the floor where I noticed he was frothing at the mouth.

I felt instinctively that I had to kneel beside him and lay my hands on his head in healing prayer, and at the same time I sought to heal any memories of his traumatic experience in his unconscious mind which might otherwise later become part of his conscious state, and so cause trouble there. I then told him to sit in his chair where I woke him from his hypnotic trance. We afterwards went for a walk and I found him to be a completely changed man. He was calm and relaxed, and remembered nothing of what had taken place. This man has never had a recurrence of his problem, and lives a normal happy life. For me it was a very wonderful experience that has been repeated many times since that day; but always there has been a deep conviction that a power greater than mine was working through me. I am assured that in the days of his flesh, Christ exercised His authority over evil; so today he manifests that authority through His Church; His power is the same, yesterday, today and forever.

I would like to give just one more example of exorcism, for the purpose of demonstrating the reality of Christ's protecting power. I had been helping a young man of nineteen years of age with a problem that worried him considerably. He had a terrible urge to interfere with small boys, and although he knew it was wrong, something seemed to be compelling him to dwell upon that thought. He came to see me on various occasions, and we talked about his problem at great length. With the help of hypnotherapy this urge gradually lessened and finally disappeared completely.

A year or so later this lad rang me again, even more frightened than before. For some time the horrible thought that he wanted to kill me kept coming into his mind. As he sat at meals and held a knife in his hand, the idea would come to him that it might be a suitable weapon with which to kill me. As he looked in at the window of a hardware shop, his eyes would fasten on to a knife, and again the frightening thought would fill his mind. All this troubled him so much that his health began to suffer; he could not sleep and lost his appetite for food. On the day he rang to tell me about his problem, he was so shocked that he had great difficulty in sharing it with me, even though he knew me so well. Or perhaps it was because he knew me. He said he felt too frightened to meet me because, as he put it, 'Something would make me kill you. I could not help myself.' After some time, I was able to persuade him to come to my home.

I realised that this was no ordinary case of mental or psychological disturbance, but that it might well be a very real devil possession; so I sought to prepare myself for whatever might happen while I awaited his arrival. I knew myself to be completely protected against anything evil could do to me, surrounded by the love and power of Christ. At that particular moment this assurance took the form of a blue light enveloping me — something that I often experience while in meditation.

When the lad arrived he seemed quite normal, and much more relaxed than he had been when speaking to me on the phone. After a brief chat, I got down to putting him under hypnosis in order to make a correct diagnosis of his condition. I had no hesitation in deciding that here was a young man who would eventually become a tool of the Devil if he was not given help at once. This may sound strange to some readers, but I had the strong conviction that the Devil had been thwarted in his attempt to destroy this lad when he tried to persuade him to interfere with little boys, and I had, as it were, come between him and his evil purpose. The logical conclusion might seem to be to destroy me. I had not long to wait before knowing the reality of evil in this young man. As soon as I began the exorcism his features became so distorted as to be barely recognisable as those of a human being. At the same time he rushed at me with a knife which he had pulled out from inside his sock under his trousers. He came to within two feet of me, then suddenly fell back in his chair, as if he had been pushed. At first I did not understand the reason, but when he did the same thing again, I began to realise what was happening. At the third attempt he collapsed on the floor — again frothing at the mouth. I was anxious to hear from him why he had not been able to reach me with that knife, so I made no attempt to heal the unconscious memory. After waking him I put that question to him, and his reply was. 'There was a wall in front of you.' He would have reacted in exactly the way he did if there had been a solid object between us. My interpretation was that the spiritual protection Christ had afforded me became for him a physical wall which prevented him from harming me.

Another instance of the evil one using human lips and actions happened when a lady of about fifty years old came to see me in a very distressed state. For many years, she had had frequent sessions when she 'lost herself', as she put it, and felt that she was 'outside' herself. I felt that there might be some unconscious psychological disturbance manifesting itself in her conscious state. Under hypnosis she told me a strange story of a previous existence when she had been born into an Italian family in Genoa. Her father in that life was a gipsy, and she had travelled around the countryside with him and the family, selling clothes pegs and the like. She talked quite freely of how her father often hit her and generally ill-treated her. The detailed way in which she described her life, and the country in which she lived, was most convincing. Then I had the idea of testing the reality of her story by asking one or two questions in Italian. To my amazement she answered them clearly and fluently in that language, which made me suppose that she was familiar with Italian. But when I later asked her about this in her conscious state, she denied that she could speak a word of the language. I continued to question her about her previous life and quite suddenly she said 'But I'm not living, you know.' This puzzled me somewhat, and when I asked her to explain what she meant by this, she said, 'I killed myself with a milk bottle.' I went no further with that investigation, but decided that evil had a part in her distress. Not that I believe that the idea of reincarnation is evil, not at all. I cannot accept the possibility of there being a previous life because I have no evidence; as far as I know the Gospels are silent on the subject. I have a completely open mind on the matter.

Before waking her from the hypnotic trance I sought to heal the memory of what she had told me, so that it would not become a part of her conscious mind. On leaving I arranged to see her again in one month. I gave her that amount of time in case she benefited from reliving those unconscious memories, though I was quite sure that eventually I should have to seek the destruction of the evil power that was the cause of her terrifying thoughts. When I met her again, I found her condition unchanged, as I had expected, and so I decided to exorcise. My main reason for quoting this case is the patient's reaction to the exorcism. She had a rather nice crucifix in her lapel, which her late mother had given her and which she valued greatly, having often talked to me about it. As I made the sign of the cross in the act of exorcism, the woman's features became so distorted as to appear to be evil personified. At the height of her frenzy she snatched at her crucifix and threw it across the room in the most vicious manner and with terrific strength.

As she collapsed into the corner of the room, I knelt beside her and laid my hands on her in healing prayer. After a few minutes she asked me what had happened to her crucifix, and I retrieved it from the opposite side of the room. On reflection it seemed as if the Devil sought to destroy the symbol of that power which was throwing him out.

Cases of possession are, thankfully, few and far between — no more than one or two a year, as far as my ministry is concerned. But another aspect of the supernatural with which

I am often confronted, and which is much more common than is generally thought to be the case, is that of the poltergeist. This phenomenon takes many forms, but I have no doubt as to the authentic nature of these manifestations.

I was once called to a house in Combe Martin where I found a lady in great distress. The family had only recently moved there, and almost every day she found items of jewellery and clothing and other things in her bedroom had been moved to other positions — so much so that she began to wonder whether or not her memory was failing.

Before taking any action I wished to satisfy myself that there really was some supernatural intervention in that room. I placed money and other items in certain positions on her dressing table along with her shoes and articles of clothing in other parts of the room; I then made a plan on paper of what I had done. I locked the bedroom door and put the key in my pocket. When we returned to the room after lunch an hour or so later, we found that the positions of the things that I had placed in various parts of the room had all been changed. Some of them had been so arranged as to give the impression that someone was playing a game and laughing at us. It was not difficult to displace that entity and so bring peace to that troubled family.

I will give just one other example of supernatural disturbance. I knew the family who called me to their home early one evening; I had often talked to them about the noises they heard at night and the feeling of a presence with them. I had taken no action up to that time, but the condition reached a climax that evening when the grandmother of the family, who lived next door, came into the home. As she turned to close the door she felt what seemed to her to be cold hands laid on her neck. She was obviously very distressed, by this, which led to me being called. I sought to comfort her, and at the same time to release the unhappy spirit, or whatever it was, in Christ's name.

That night the family had peace, but there was worse to come the next morning. The mother had gone into the sitting room to clear out the fire grate, and having removed the hearth rug and fender, she began to rake out the ashes when she was called by her daughter to the kitchen for a cup of coffee. Some ten minutes or so later she returned to the sitting room to find utter chaos. Half the hearth tiles had been dug up, broken into hundreds of tiny pieces, much too small to replace, and put into a neat pile in the corner of the room. She was so shocked that she left the room at once and telephoned me. If I had not seen that damage and knew the integrity of the people concerned, I would not have believed it possible for such damage to be done without any sound. The tiles were firmly fixed, and would have needed an iron bar to remove them, quite apart from the breaking of them which would normally create quite a noise. This remains for me one of the imponderables of my life, but at the same time, it emphasised for me the reality of the spiritual dimension which is able to overshadow the physical.

A year after our second canal holiday, Sir Dennis Stucley very kindly offered us a two-week holiday in his little cottage at Blackpool Mill in Hartland. This old building had recently been restored and was let each summer as furnished holiday accommodation. I am sure Sir Dennis will never fully appreciate the joy that he gave to Dorothy and me by this generous offer: to be able to spend two weeks at a spot that held such happy memories; to awake again in my beloved Hartland with the sound of the waves breaking on the beach where I had spent so many happy hours when young. That holiday more than lived up to our expectations, and was the beginning of a yearly pilgrimage until my retirement. The cottage is situated only twenty yards from the water's edge in a beautiful valley. Each year the weather was kind to us and on a balmy late May morning there is nowhere that I would wish to be more than at Blackpool Mill. To walk across that soft springy turf in the early morning and over the pebbled beach to plunge into the Atlantic breakers is a most exhilarating experience — sufficient to destroy any tension or stress of life in the parishes after only two or three days.

During those holidays we enjoyed the walks with our dogs along the paths we had trodden before we were married forty years earlier and recalled all the happy memories. Trees on which I had carved my initials nearly sixty years before hardly seemed to have changed at all — still sturdy and reliable as I had thought them to be when a child, reminding me of the unchanging nature of their creator. Those paths also took us along the banks of the lovely stream which twists and gurgles its way through that valley over a series of waterfalls into the sea, and where the trout would be leaping in the early morning sunshine before settling under the stones on the bed of the stream to rest for the day. Here, too, the flycatchers and wagtails would be darting up and down, breakfasting on the myriads of insects hovering over the water.

After a day of walking or sitting beside the stream, catching up on my much neglected reading or in meditation, and a lovely meal to end the day, we used to sit on the cliff to watch the sun disappearing over the horizon of the ocean, as it had done hundreds of times since I last witnessed it in my young days at Newton. Then we would climb the rickety old staircase to bed — to a sleep that I can only describe as child-like; our last thoughts being of thankfulness to our dear friends who had made such ecstasy possible.

One of the greatest joys of our holidays at Hartland was the opportunity to worship again in the church where we had shared so many happy experiences. During those services I often used to wonder what difference it would have made to our lives if I had accepted the bishop's invitation to become vicar of that parish. But I knew that any doubts that still lingered were of a sentimental nature, and that deep down I was still convinced I had made the right decision.

It was good, too, to be sharing with many old friends in worship after so many years, though they were by that time far fewer in number, and they had, like myself, 'changed with the changing years'. I had been back from time to time, to assist in laying to rest a loved one or a colleague from former days, but to worship there on holiday was something quite different. At the first Eucharist after so long, I experienced a sense of completeness I had never known before. I knew that all whom I had known and loved in that parish, and who were in the nearer presence of God, together with those at that service, were gathered up, as it were, into the person of Christ, where time and space have no meaning, and where the Divine Consciousness of God alone is reality.

During our holidays each year at that wonderful spot, I had an opportunity to renew my acquaintance with Hartland Abbey, where I had spent so many happy hours as a boy. Dorothy visited the buildings for the first time when we went there for a meal with our friends during our stay, but she soon came to love and enjoy the beauty of the place as much as I did. The gardens, too, were a source of much pleasure to us, and we spent many pleasant afternoons there. Sir Dennis and Lady Stucley had greatly improved the grounds since coming there to live in the early thirties. The camellias, rhododendrons and azaleas were in full bloom each time we went on holiday and they gave us much joy.

In 1971 we had our usual holiday at Blackpool Mill in May, but that summer and early autumn I had a particularly difficult time in the parishes, so I decided to have a retreat alone at the cottage in the autumn. I took the dog for company, and did not see another human being during that time. Because the weather had by then changed to rain and gales, I was able to spend my time in front of a blazing log fire, by exactly the same type of open fireplace I had known as a boy. This proved to be a most therapeutic experience, during which time I was able to relax completely, in wonderful peace and tranquillity, to readjust myself in readiness to tackle whatever problems lay ahead back home in the parishes.

There the usual round of activities continued, and looking at my diary for any one of those years is an interesting, if nostalgic, exercise. The days seem to have been so fully occupied that one wonders how time was found for the many things that are not recorded day by day, such as house-to-house visiting and sermon preparation. Surely there can be no more fascinating, interesting and rewarding work than that of a parish priest. I know that 'my lot was set in a fair country', and that it might have been different had I been called to a parish in an industrial area.

As a parish priest I often sat at a death bed. One such occasion left a deep impression on me. A lady of about fifty years of age was in a coma, and her doctor had said that she was unlikely to recover. I was sitting beside her bed holding her hand, while her family sat around the room, waiting for the end. After half an hour or so I felt impelled to lay on the bed beside the sick person and hold her in my arms while at the same time loving her in Christ. I felt that His healing love and power was being manifested in that lady; that my arms were as His arms. Her breathing was very irregular and at times almost non-existent. I remained in that position for nearly an hour, and then I felt a wonderful glow in my arms. At the same time the patient's breathing pattern changed: it became even and light. I knew that something wonderful had happened, so I released my arms and discovered that she was sleeping as peacefully as a baby. She woke after about five hours and within a few weeks she was quite normal.

On another occasion a girl of about thirteen was in a coma. Her mother had died some two or three years previously. I was sitting beside the bed holding her hand in silent prayer, when she suddenly sat up, held out her arms and exclaimed, 'Mummy, Mummy!' Then she fell back and died. The wonderful thing about this incident was the look of recognition in this child's eyes and the joy on her face; it was as if she saw her mother coming in the bedroom door. I felt quite sure that she had had a very real vision of an existence beyond this physical life.

As time went on I was frequently invited to speak about the Ministry of Healing to groups outside my own diocese. This later developed into regular clinics in these places, where I sought to help people with their problems. As a result I have many dear friends in other parts of the country with whom I am privileged to share in the deeper realities of the spiritual life.

My relationship with doctors had widened down the years and gone beyond my local practice to other parts of North Devon, where I met some dedicated Christian doctors who saw my work as a contribution to their work of healing. As a result of this I had the privilege of sharing with the bishop in a series of post-graduate lectures. This afforded us a grand opportunity to share with those young men and women who had recently qualified as doctors something of our thoughts and aspirations for the place of spiritual healing in their work in the future. I was very impressed with the attitude of those young people towards our work, and the openness of their minds towards the spiritual in the field of wholeness. There is certainly a wind of change taking place in the thinking of the medical profession with regard to the Church's Ministry of Healing. The dogmatic, materialistic and purely scientific attitude of the older doctors is giving way to an acceptance by many younger people of the place of the spiritual dimension in their profession.

Of all the cases of disease with which I am confronted in my ministry, the most frustrating, and yet most interesting, is that of cancer in its various forms. I know that in most cases people turn to Divine help as a last resort, when it is often too late. I know nothing of medicine, but I have often wondered if cancer is different from other diseases in that it is something that multiplies and grows. I believe that all sickness is 'of the Devil' — that is to say, it is contrary to God's perfect will; but cancer seems to be an especially evil thing. I have from time to time sought to treat cancer as being a type of possession, with some success. I remember being called to a lady who was in the last stages of a carcinoma of the oesophagus. Of all the cases I have sought to help, I think this must be the most tragic. The lady's husband had had a tumour on the brain for several years and was almost a 'cabbage'. Her eldest son appeared to be fit and well, but the second son had had a leg amputated at the knee because of cancer in the bone marrow. The next son seemed to enjoy good health, but the youngest boy aged five years had been born with a tumour on the brain, and had spent longer in comas than in a conscious state since his birth. The mother had been given but a few days to live when I saw her, having taken no solid food for three months because she was unable to swallow.

She had had a terrible childhood, having witnessed her father murder her mother, and had gone through a period of great stress during her teenage years. She had suffered much at the hands of her husband who had become very violent at times. Despite all this, she was one of the brightest, most positive thinking people I have ever met. Even in her obvious physical weakness she still sought to look to the future, and to plan for her family.

The day I visited her was just two days before she was due to see her consultant, whom she had seen a month earlier. After a long talk about the love and healing purpose of God through Jesus Christ, she became so sure that she was going to be made whole that she could hardly wait for me to begin my ministration. Terribly weak as she was, her mind was fully alert and anxious to co-operate with me. I had talked to her about my thoughts on the evil of cancer and the place of exorcism, and went on to explain to her what I intended to do. I do not normally experience any supernatural power being present at a time like this, but on this occasion I was aware of a tremendous strength that seemed to overwhelm us. I was convinced after that exorcism, and when I had laid my hands on her head in healing prayer, that she was healed. I had no physical evidence for this; she herself felt no different than she had before I came to her. I left her with the promise that she would get her son to phone me with the result of her visit to her consultant.

A very excited young man rang me two days later to say that his mother had been told that the cancer had completely disappeared. I went to see her the next day, and she told me that her consultant had had her X-rayed and examined her himself. He then called his medical staff and senior nursing staff to look at the plates and at her throat. He told them that one month previously she had a terminal carcinoma of the oesophagus, but now it had completely gone. He then asked her what had happened since he last saw her, and she told him that she had seen me. He then told her to go to see me again, and if possible stay at my home in order that

I might teach her to swallow. This she did for two or three days, and went home radiantly whole and happy. Neither did she keep her good news to herself, but was the means of bringing many people to Christ by her witness, including two doctors who had witnessed her wonderful healing through His power.

But an even more wonderful example of His healing touch was yet to be revealed in that family. I visited the home a few weeks after the mother had been healed, and was talking to her; the youngest boy with the tumour on the brain was sitting in a chair opposite me. He looked a pathetic little figure, like a child from a concentration camp of the last war. His head had been shaved for the treatment he had had, and his huge dark eyes seemed to be constantly fixed on me. As I talked to his mother about her wonderful experience, I was conscious of his gaze. After several minutes he got off his chair and staggered towards me, barely able to stand up. He laid his head on my knees and looking up into my face, he said, 'Kiss my head better for Jesus.' I was very taken aback; I had not heard him speak before, but I quickly pulled myself together and laid my hands on his head in healing prayer: then I bent and kissed him in Christ's name. From then on we had to restrain his talking — he just went on and on. He asked me to pick him up in my arms and carry him around the room, looking at the pictures, most of which were of bible stories. He put his finger on each one, and excitedly shouted, 'Jesus, Jesus!' Again, I experienced a tremendous joy in that room. I felt sure that something wonderful had happened. It was as if it had been Christ who had been carrying that little lad around that room; Christ who had laid His hands upon him and kissed him, not myself. The result of all that was that child was healed of the brain tumour.

People are often referred to me after dabbling with an ouija board; that is a form of spiritualistic seance, where a board lettered with the alphabet and other signs is used with a movable pointer by which messages are written. Some of these people, often quite young, spend many hours with these things, with frightening consequences.

I remember being called to Bideford at two o'clock in the morning by a young man, who, between his screams and unrepeatable language, begged me to come and help him. When I arrived I found six teenagers who had been playing with an ouija board for the whole of the previous weekend. They were running up and down the Quay, screaming and shouting. One of their number, a girl, ran off in an hysterical state, and I did not see her again. The police came to see what it was all about, so I bundled the remaining five into my car and took them to the home of one of the girls. Her parents left their bed amidst the noise and confusion, and made us coffee. I saw each of the teenagers separately, and talked of the danger their action could have involved them in, and the possible consequences. These young people were not possessed in any sense, but by their action they were opening themselves to that possibility. As they watched that board hour after hour, their minds became a vacuum, open to influence; then it is that evil so often takes over. I talked to them about the love and power of Christ as opposed to that of evil and what His power could do in their lives if they would allow Him to take over. We finished at about 5 am when two of the lads came to thank me for helping them all, and with a request 'to know more about this Lord Jesus you have been talking about'. I was able to put them in touch with their parish priest, and they later became members of his prayer group.

All through my ministry I have had a deep desire to have a home of healing; that is to say, a house large enough to accommodate eight or ten people at a time who needed spiritual or psychological help — perhaps before going into hospital, or those who have just been discharged and need help in rehabilitation. Then there is the young mother who has become worn down by the demands of her family, and needs somewhere to relax and recuperate so as to be able to stand back and look at life more objectively. I have felt for many years that there are people in need of such help, which hospitals cannot provide, but which would be a real form of preventive medicine — thus easing the pressure upon the medical profession. We have tried to do something along these lines in our own parsonage houses, and have been wonderfully blessed. Perhaps that is the way God wanted us to do it rather than on a bigger scale.

21

Farewell to Exmoor

Life on my beloved Exmoor pursued its relentless course. The good and the bad seasons for farmers; the broken marriages, and those which, together with God, we were able to repair. The heartbreak of parents whose teenage boy or girl had 'gone off the rails', and the wonderful joy when the prodigal returned. Then too, even in the midst of such beautiful surroundings there was the deeply depressed parishioner, and even the suicide and the sudden death that deeply shocked the caring neighbours. The call to the hospital at two o'clock in the morning to baptise the baby who was not expected to live because it had been born with only one kidney, and that not functioning normally; the heartache of that young mother as I exhorted her to give that little one back to God, in her heart, which she did; and the joy of seeing that baby grow up into a strong healthy lad, and his mother into a dedicated servant of Christ.

All this, and so much more was my

wonderful privilege and honour as I sought to be the parson — God's person — in that lovely part of His vineyard. But little by little there was dawning on me the fact that I was trying to do two jobs, and perhaps not doing either in the way God would have me do them. More and more people were coming from far afield, seeking help with all kinds of problems. Should I refuse to see them and concentrate solely on the parishes, where a great deal of the work was of an administrative nature, but all of which I enjoyed so much? Or should I consider relinquishing parochial work completely and giving my full time to the Ministry of Healing?

This was the dilemma I faced for the next year or so. I was then nearly sixty-five years old, and if I could find a house to rent, I could then claim my state pension. But my clergy pension would be small because I would not have completed my full forty years. Added to that I would have no travelling allowance from any source, the diocese having refused to grant me anything because, it was said, my work would not be of an official nature. I knew that on that very limited income, we should not find it easy to 'make both ends meet', and also do the work I wished to do. It was at this time that Dorothy had to go into hospital for a major operation, so I took no further action on a decision about our future, but continued to seek God's guidance on it. Thankfully Dorothy made a successful recovery, but during her convalescence, I had a letter from the archdeacon offering me the parsonage house at Woolsery, near Bideford, with the invitation to look after the parish of Hartland during an interregnum.

Here, indeed, was perhaps the greatest quandary I had ever been in. I was being offered a very nice bungalow with four bedrooms, large enough for our family and with room to accommodate people in need of the help God would have me give. It was not where I had hoped to live in retirement, but at the same time only four miles distant there was the added incentive, as it were, of being able to minister in the parish and the church that meant so much to me. It was as if God was compensating me for the disappointment when I declined the bishop's invitation to accept that living many years before. But I was still not sure this move would be right, and still more important was the fact that Dorothy did not want to go there; this made me wonder if it was God's will. There was a great deal of prayer and discussion but eventually we decided to accept and leave our lovely home and the people of Exmoor.

As with all our moves, it was the tearing of ourselves away from those wonderful people that hurt us so much. We had spent eleven happy years in those parishes — years which seemed to have been no longer than months. Again there was to be the heartache of farewells in each parish and these were made all the harder by a feeling of doubt as to whether I had chosen to go for sentimental reasons because of the chance of working in my home parish for a while. However, out of all these thoughts there finally emerged the conviction that Dorothy would eventually be happy in our new home, and that since we were soon to reach the age of retirement anyway, here was a house suitable for the work which I was so sure God still wanted me to do for Him.

It would be foolish of me even to try to name all the faithful souls whose lives touched ours during our time in those Exmoor parishes. I had seen babies whom I had baptised, eventually confirmed; what greater joy could have been mine than to see those little ones come to years of discretion, and so take upon themselves the task of following Christ in the promise that had been made on their behalf at their baptism.

I had prepared so many young couples for marriage and seen the excitement in their faces as they sat hand in hand, listening to what I had to say to them. Then I shared the joy of their wedding day and had the privilege of watching them settle down to married life, and sometimes the responsibility of seeking to help and guide them with their early problems.

The occasions when I seemed to have been closest to my people were during bereavements: the death of a beautiful teenage girl — an only child — whose parents had had little time for the things of the spirit, but who came to know Christ in the most wonderful way as a result of their terrible loss. Then there was dear Ethel Smith, a wonderful Christian lady whom everyone in North Molton loved deeply, who had taught at the village school for more than forty years and later helped with my Sunday school; when she was laid to rest at the age of eighty-seven, we all knew that a saint had passed from our midst.

Not least of those to whom I owe a debt of gratitude are the church-wardens and members of the church councils of the three parishes. The councils had obviously changed their membership down the years, but there were three wardens who had welcomed me into those parishes still in office, and who had been such a support to me throughout my ministry there: Henry Ayre at North Molton; Harry Thorne at Twitchen and Ron Crook at Molland. Thank you all, my friends, for just being you.

Then there were those other dear souls whom we find in every parish: humble, sincere, faithful people who were to be found in their place at almost every service in church or at prayer groups, or when there was work to be done for Christ in the parishes. They never pushed themselves forward into the limelight; they would not even be found on church councils. I thank God for every remembrance of them; it was often their integrity and faithfulness that buoyed me up when things were difficult.

The dreaded day of farewells came all too quickly upon us. For the last time I celebrated the Holy Communion in each of those churches. For the last time Dorothy and I stood at the doors to say goodbye to the dear people of whom we felt so much a part. They, too, showed their love and sorrow by their wonderful farewell gifts and their tears.

We ended our stay at North Molton in the way we had begun it — by spending an evening with Maurice and Joan Whinney and the church council at Holridge, where we had a most wonderful farewell party. I officially retired on the Saturday evening before leaving the following Monday, so that although we were still living in the vicarage, I was no longer vicar and could not celebrate Holy Communion at either of the churches. This fact hit me very hard; the thought that never again would I be parish priest but only be able to help in time of need. This made me feel very humble and brought me down from my pedestal with a bang. I remember going to Holy Communion that Sunday morning, feeling much closer to God because of that experience, and so grateful for all his mercies granted to me during my years in those parishes.

22

Old Birds Come Home to Roost

With very heavy hearts we left for our new home at Woolsery — neither of us quite sure if we were doing the right thing. We did not expect anyone to meet us when we arrived, because we were coming into that parish as private citizens. But to our amazement and great joy, there were three parishioners awaiting our arrival to help unload our furniture, and their wives were ready to provide us with all kinds of refreshment. It was a most wonderful welcome, and we are proud to call them friends.

We had a very testing time in the early weeks of my retirement. Dorothy became very depressed, because she had not fully recovered from her operation, and because our new home was in an isolated position meant that she saw very few people. This was in sharp contrast to our vicarage at North Molton in the middle of a large village, with people coming in and out all day long. The girls, too, who were by this time thirteen and fourteen years old, found it anything but easy to adapt to their new school, after having just happily settled into the South Molton secondary modern school. It was difficult for them to leave all the friends they had made during their young lives.

My unhappiness was greatly tempered by the fact that the following week I was to take over responsibility for the parish where I had been born and brought up, and of which I felt very much a part. I was a little apprehensive for some strange reason; I could hardly believe it was true. On that Sunday morning I set off for Welcombe, a little village on the Cornish boundary adjoining Hartland, with which it is held in plurality; here I felt quite happy. Perhaps this was because I had not worshipped there very often in former days, and also because only two or three members of the congregation were known to me. I was given a wonderful reception by that little company, whom I later came to know and love.

From there I went on to Hartland parish church about seven miles away — a journey I shall never forget. It was a beautiful May morning and I was travelling along roads I knew so well and which I had traversed so many times in the years gone by. All the way I had a terrible feeling of inadequacy — almost of dread. I was warmly welcomed by the wardens, my friend Sir Dennis Stucley, who was often in my former congregation at North Molton, and Horace Prust, who had been an old school pal. All this helped a great deal, but still there remained the strange feeling that I should be in a pew and not leading the worship of the people. It was a Holy Communion service, and as I stood at the altar it was as if I was in a dream, and that what was happening was not real. The familiar layout of the building, the furniture and fittings, the vestments and communion vessels all seemed to take me back over forty years in time. But perhaps the most peculiar sensation was that my dear old friend and vicar of those far off days was there with me at the altar, and I felt very unworthy. Then I became conscious of his smiling approval, which gave me great encouragement. From then on I knew that all was well, and that I should really enjoy my ministry in my home parish.

As the weeks and months passed by, I began to realise that my fears about ministering to men and women with whom I had been brought up was not nearly as difficult as I had expected. Of course I was not their vicar, and so had no authority in running the affairs of the church and parish. But they accepted me as their priest, and sought my help and advice, just as they would from any other priest.

It gave me great joy, too, to visit many old friends in that capacity, though for a while this also seemed strange. I remember the first time I went back to my old home at Newton after coming back to Hartland as their priest, I had the same sensations as when I stood at the altar in church. The twenty-seven years I had lived there seemed to spread out before me, with all the happiness that had been mine. I felt that faces of so many dear ones, long since passed to their rest, appeared to be all around me. In all this there was nothing of sentiment, just a tremendous surge of thankfulness and joy. Added to this was the wonderful affection with which my dear friends at Newton welcomed me home.

I often visited a home where I had known a school friend; I was met one day by a young man who looked very like my old friend and whom I took to be his son, only to discover that he was my friend's grandson. Such is the speed of time, but thankfully our minds do not dwell too closely on the passing years. At baptisms and weddings, too, I was constantly being brought up against the fact that I was now two generations from where I had been when I left Hartland. Before the Second World War, the great majority of the people who lived in Hartland had been born and brought up in that parish. When I returned as a priest I found a large number of people who, in my young days, would have been called 'foreigners' — most of them people who had been in the habit of taking their annual holidays there, and who had come to love the place. When they retired they had decided to make their home where they had known so much happiness, and I found their contribution to the life of that parish to be of tremendous importance.

As the great festivals of the Church came round, each brought with it some happy memory for me. I felt deeply thankful to those who had taught me so much of the Christian faith, and whose lives had influenced mine many years before. One such occasion was Remembrance Sunday; and here I must confess, a little sentimentality did enter in. It was when I had to read the names of those who had been killed in the Second World War that I was so touched. Of course I had heard the long list of names of those who had given their lives in the First World War read out many times, and I knew two or three of them. But here were the names of those with whom I had played as a child and worked with as a man — some of whom I did not even know had been killed. All of which only emphasised more deeply in my mind the sheer evil and waste of war.

Because we had come to live so near to Blackpool Mill, Dorothy and I often went there, and to Hartland Abbey. On one such visit Sir Dennis Stucley talked to me about the possibility of arranging conducted tours of the Abbey for interested groups of people. I thought this was a wonderful idea; apart from the history of the building itself, there are so many interesting things inside, so I gladly agreed to help him; I knew the old place so well, and would enjoy sharing it with others.

So almost every week since then, during the summer months Dorothy and I share with Sir Dennis and Lady Stucley in these conducted tours around their beautiful home and gardens.

My time as priest-in-charge of Hartland passed all too quickly. In just over a year an appointment was made to the parish, which gave me great joy. A young man was instituted as vicar who could not have pleased me more if I had made the choice myself. The result has been that I have found a young friend who supports me in my work, and with whom I find pleasure in sharing in his ministry. Long may Louis Coulson continue to be vicar of my beloved parish.

Within two weeks of being released from responsibility for Hartland, the incumbent of Woolsery where we live, together with Clovelly and Bucks Mills, resigned, and I was asked to take over these three parishes. I found this to be very frustrating. I had retired from the parochial ministry in order to concentrate on my work in healing, but now I was unable to expand in that direction. I had continued to seek to help a few people in my home each week since leaving North Molton, apart from attending to the needs of the parishioners of Hartland; but again for an indefinite period I should have to restrict that work. I tried to accept this as God's will, and that there was a purpose to it, but all the while there was the thought that I could be doing just the same work back in the parishes on Exmoor, where for the past year they had had no vicar. I think Dorothy felt this even more acutely than I, because she had been unable to settle happily in our new home.

So it was that I found myself in a similar situation to the one I had left a little more than a year earlier: three churches, three parochial church councils; in short, three of everything, plus many problems, the like of which I had never met in any parish in which I have ever ministered. This was to continue for the next two years, and these were to be the most unhappy years of my ministry.

It seemed as if an appointment to this group of parishes would never be made. Eight men came and looked and for various reasons 'passed by on the other side'. But at last I feel sure the parishes have the right man, and I know that I have a colleague whom I have come to know and love and in whose company and fellowship I find great joy. Again I can say, long may Derek Bates be the incumbent of these parishes, and I thank God for the privilege that he gives me in sharing in his ministry.

At last by 1980 I was free to give my full time to the work I love most, without the responsibility of the parishes. It was good not to have to refuse to see dear souls because of some administrative commitment. Again I was able to accept referrals from doctors and clergy, and so to do what I believe God has called me to do in my latter years. But I could do none of this without the love and support of my dear wife. Throughout my ministry she has called herself the 'Martha' of the team, but only God and I know how much my Martha has contributed to any success that has been granted to our team effort in Christ. Apart from her special work with the foster children after our own had grown up, and all these young girls who came to us so broken-hearted, and in need of a mother's love, there have also been the emergencies. The frequent call in the early hours of the morning from the police: 'We have a young woman here with her baby who has been thrown out of her home by her drunken husband. Can you take her into your home for the night?' I would go off to Barnstaple to fetch the poor frightened little soul, perhaps dressed in only her nightdress and slippers on a winter's night, and Dorothy would get busy making up a bed and preparing a hot meal.

When I have had to sit up all night with a teenager suffering 'cold turkey' Dorothy would see to it that I was refreshed from time to time with cups of tea. Or there would be the telephone call from many miles away: 'My wife (or husband) is on the verge of a nervous breakdown. Can you please have her in your home to help her?' That person could not be healed without Dorothy's help. I could go on quoting innumerable examples of my wife's wonderful contribution to my ministry, without which it would have been the poorer, and I know of many priests whose ministries have been enriched by such support from a loving partner.

23

The Joy of Retirement

So the years roll on — every hour filled with a great sense of happiness as one sees dear souls made whole, or start on that road through the love and power of Christ in their lives. One of my greatest joys has been the simplicity and the naturalness of that love and power at work, as I have watched unwholesome lives begin to blossom again, often after many years of unhappiness or sickness of body, mind or spirit, in some cases where they have never before known a full and radiant life.

When a person comes to a realisation of the fact that 'I can of mine own self do nothing', and puts it into practice every waking moment, by letting God take over, only then does that person begin to live. Too many people lay their emphasis on two opposing forces — good and evil. They seek a God who will provide all the good things they need, and who will destroy the things that hurt them. It is not God's power to provide nor His power to destroy that we should seek, but God himself. God is not a power to give or take away; a God who is a good power or a bad power, but a creative, maintaining and sustaining power. When a person comes to that way of thinking, he or she really has to acknowledge, 'I can of mine own self do nothing, but in Christ I can do all things'.

I have discovered that it is only when we are ready to give up our own ideas about God, to stop thinking and planning what we ought to do or ought not to do, only in that complete surrender can God reveal Himself to us. God can only reveal Himself in the wholeness of our lives, as we acknowledge that He is; that He is Divine Adjustment; that He is Perfect Everything. That is what the Ministry of Healing is all about.

This does not mean we can just sit back and do nothing; we seek His will and co-operate with that will, seeking to create these conditions to enable His will to be done. I am reminded of the corny old joke about the vicar who was visiting a parishioner one summer's evening and found him working in his garden. In the course of conversation the Vicar said that he hoped the man realised that it was only God who could bring a harvest out of the garden. The old man paused for a moment, and then replied 'Before I came to live here twenty years ago,

God had this garden all to Himself, but there wasn't much of a harvest.'

Yes, God needs our co-operation: 'Without God, we cannot. Without us, God will not.' That co-operation must be according to His perfect laws, and that means placing our whole being — body, mind and spirit, within that perfection so that His mind becomes our mind, and His will, our will. We need, too, to give Him not only ourselves, but our sins, our diseases, our fears, our health and our wealth, that He may take them all. We ask just one gift in return — the gift of Himself, to love and enjoy Him forever. That is the life He intends for us; that is the abundant life He promised for us. In every person who comes to me, I see something more of the reality of God, a little more of the depth of His love and compassion as they come to accept that wonderful life.

Since my retirement from the parochial ministry, and apart from the thirty or so people who come to see me each week with various problems, I have set myself two widely diverse but very interesting subjects to explore. In the first of these I am seeking to learn more about the fascinating subject of hypnotherapy and its application in life. I never cease to wonder at the complexity of the unconscious mind, and the complications that so often occur in life as a result of the unhealed memories and wounds it contains.

I am convinced that there are many people struggling with problems which make their lives nothing better than a miserable existence, and for whom drugs are not the answer. These so often only touch the symptoms, and the cause remains. Many such people have lived with these conditions most of their lives, and have come to see them as the norm. A young man of nineteen years once came to me with a problem that had troubled him for as long as he could remember, but he thought it was 'just one of those things,' as he put it, with which he had to live. He had always resented anyone resting their hand or arm upon his shoulder; if another lad wrestled with him in fun, John, as I shall call him, had been known to suddenly lash out with his fists in the most vicious way, often causing damage. Everyone thought it was sheer bad temper, and he himself had come to accept it as such. John could not make any sort of relationship with a girl; if any girl so much as laid a hand on his shoulder, he immediately left her. He always wore clothes that were too large for him, because he could not bear to feel them pressing against his body: the wearing of a collar and tie was an impossibilty. As a schoolboy the authorities had sought to compel him to do this with disastrous results.

This condition was obviously making this young man's life intolerable. He had been prescribed sedatives for years but with negative results. In talking to him I could find nothing that might have brought about this condition, so I decided to regress him while he was under hypnosis, to find out what his unconscious contained. It was not until I had talked him back through his life to the age of two years that I began to get some idea of what had brought about those horrible reactions. In one of those sessions I took the place of his mother, and suggested to him that he was a small baby, and that I was putting him in his cot and tucking the blankets around him. At that point he reacted violently. He began to scream, 'Mummy, Mummy, don't tuck me up so tightly. I can't breathe, I can't move.' His arms flailed and his face became more and more red, while the perspiration stood up on his forehead.

There was no doubt that when that lad felt the pressure of someone's arm on his shoulder, tight clothes or a tie around his neck, the wound of the unconscious memory of his mother tucking him up so tightly, opened up, as it were, and brought about the reaction. In all such cases I seek to heal that memory, first by suggesting to the unconscious that the memory will never again be manifested in his conscious state; in other words, that the wound may be healed. I always follow this by laying my hands on the subject's head in prayer, seeking Christ's healing touch — He who alone is the healer. That young man is now living a full and happy life, not having had a reaction since that day.

Another condition in which I have been privileged to have a great deal of a success is that of anorexia nervosa. It is very important that I have the patient in my home during the period of treatment, because their eating habits need to be carefully watched.

In the process of hypnotising a person, the voice plays a part, obviously, because one suggests that the subject is feeling tired and the limbs are getting heavy, and so on. But more important than the voice for a really successful hypnotist is the mind, which is projected to the mind of the subject, willing him or her to feel or to be or do this or that. I discovered several years ago that it is possible to put a person under hypnosis when he or she is not present with me, but in another room. This is made much easier when that person has been previously subjected to hypnotism, although this is not always necessary. I suppose this method would be called mind projection or telepathy.

I remember coming home in a train with a colleague from London when a young man began to make a nuisance of himself and disturbed other people in the carriage. My friend suggested that I 'put him to sleep' as he termed it. I agreed and without speaking, because he was at the far end of the carriage, I concentrated my mind upon his mind and willed him to sit down. Then I put him into a normal hypnotic state. He 'slept' quietly until just before reaching Taunton when the horrible thought occured to me that maybe he had needed to leave the train at an earlier station. I 'woke' him in the same way before I left the train, and he seemed quite happy and relaxed. I have often wondered whether some such exercise might be possible in dealing with those people who hold others as hostages, though I imagine they might not prove to be very good subjects. It would indeed be a wonderful answer to a frightening problem.

Hypnotherapy in the right hands can be, and is, a wonderfully therapeutic medium. I have worked in this field for some forty years, but not until about ten years ago did it occur to me that it could have evil consequences when used to wrong ends. A psychiatrist in

Wales referred a patient to me who was a school teacher, and who had lost the ability to write, either with chalk on a blackboard, or with a pen or pencil on paper. The psychiatrist told me that he considered the problem to be psychosomatic in origin, which meant that the man's mind was saying as it were 'You cannot hold a piece of chalk or a pen or a pencil' and the body was responding to that suggestion. There was no physiological explanation for this man's inability to write.

This was a simple case of impressing upon the unconscious mind the fact that he could write in the normal way, and with the man under hypnosis, I did just that. Before waking him I gave him a child's blackboard and a piece of chalk and asked him to write his name. This he did in quite a legible hand, even though his eyes were closed. I then healed the memory so that he would not remember writing his name.

Something that I do not fully understand is how a subject under hypnosis is able to write so legibly with his eyes shut. It would seem that he 'sees' with his mind. This man's signature could not have been more clear if he had written it when fully awake. When I 'woke' him I suggested that he should write his name, and gave him the same blackboard and chalk. On seeing his signature, he exclaimed, 'Good God, when did I write that?' After I had explained the facts to him, he again wrote his name, and it was identical to that written when he was under hypnosis. Then it was that I suddenly realised the implications of such a situation. In the wrong hands that session could have been used to get the man to put his signature to all kinds of documents and cheques — without his knowledge, but with disastrous results.

Most of my work in hypnotherapy is of a much less dramatic nature, being mainly concerned in helping people suffering with nervous conditions or with phobias and obsessions. I see many people who wish to stop smoking or are suffering from obesity; of these over 90 per cent are successfully helped. I believe this therapy to be very important, it being preventative medicine.

My second interest in retirement is a study of St Nectan and his life at Hartland, along with that of the inhabitants of the parish up to the time the monks came to the Abbey in 1160. Since leaving my home parish in 1938 a very interesting little book called *The Life of St Nectan* has been published; it was written by the late Reverend Gilbert H. Doble. I found this to be an absorbing book which brings to life, as it were, the old stories I had heard when a boy in that parish, and which always fascinated me so much.

* * *

I began my story by saying how fortunate I was to be born in such a beautiful part of the world, and into such a loving family. On reading that story now, I realise how very much more fortunate I have been in being influenced and supported by the multitude of dear souls whose lives have touched mine. I am humbled, too, by the privilege that has been mine in being a channel for so many who needed Christ's healing touch, but God alone knows what a blessing each one of them has been to me.

My prayer is that someone, after reading this simple life story, may feel drawn to give themselves to Christ — humble plough boy or girl though they may be — and allow Him to take their lives to 'break them, make them, and mould them', to be and to do that which is His will.

Notes on the History of Hartland Abbey

Hartland Abbey was built during the twelfth century and consecrated by Bishop Bartholomew of Exeter in 1160 as a monastery of the Regular Canons of the Order of St Augustine of Hippo, to serve the parish church of St Nectan. The foundation of the Abbey originated through the gift of Lord Dynham, Lord of the Manor of Hartland, and a representative of the Norman family who took over this area after the Norman Conquest. There is an inscription on the wall outside the drawing room window, dated 1310, which records Monk John of Exeter as having repaired the cloisters.

The Abbey was occupied by the monks from 1160 to 1540. When Henry VIII dissolved the monasteries and seized the church lands in 1536, he gave the Abbey and the lands to a Mr William Abbott who was his Sergeant of the Cellar at Hampton Court. Records show that at the time of the dissolution there were only about six monks in residence at the Abbey.

During the four hundred years of its occupation by the monks, the Abbey was not only the centre of religious life in Hartland, but because the monks were probably the only educated people in the district, they would have looked after legal problems and given the lead in agricultural matters as well as being generally responsible for the welfare of the people round about. They did much to make our countryside as beautiful as it is when they enclosed the fields, using the stumps of trees from the forest which had been cut down to make the hedges — so retaining the great variety of woodland trees we see in our hedges today. Many of these fields were probably named by the monks: names like Church Park, Broken Cross and Monks Close.

After Mr Abbott took possession of the Abbey it became a private residence, and it has never been sold since that time, but interestingly has passed down three times through the female line. The Abbey was built across the valley as it stands today; part of the present building is, in fact, constructed upon the foundations and basement walls of the original house, while on the west side part of the old house remains. In the days of the monks it covered a much greater area. The Great Hall went out at right angles from the south end of the main house in an easterly direction. The Abbey chapel extended at right angles from the north end of the house, thus forming three sides of a square with a courtyard in the middle.

I remember my grandfather showing me an opening to a tunnel which his men had started to dig on the instructions of Sir Lewis Stucley, the owner of the Abbey at that time, believing that it led to the parish church which the monks served. He told me that it had been beautifully built but that the roots of the large trees above it had caused the roof to become dangerous, so Sir Lewis abandoned the work. I have often wondered if the monks really did use that tunnel and who dug it and built it: it would certainly have been a great asset to them in getting to and from the church where they did a twenty-four hour stint, carrying out the seven statutory services each day. There is a small room over the north porch of the church, known as Pope's chamber, where the monks on duty would have rested between services. It was probably named after Monk Pope, who was the senior monk at the time of the dissolution.

As I wandered around the Abbey when I was young, I used to wonder at what stage in its history the sound of children's voices first rang through those corridors. Obviously they were not heard for the first four hundred years: the only sounds in the valley during that time would have been the cawing of rooks as they nested in the huge oak trees, just as they do today. The monks would probably have kept a few cows to provide dairy produce, and apart from their bovine noises, silence would have reigned supreme.

When William Abbott arrived, everything was changed and there were children running around, but by 1600 there was no son to carry on the family name, only a daughter called Catherine. She eventually married Nicholas Luttrell of Dunster Castle, near Minehead in Somerset. The Abbey remained in that family name for the next hundred years, and then again there was no son to keep the family name going. Once more history repeated itself, and a daughter, Mary, was the eligible heiress. She married Paul Orchard, a son of Charles Orchard of Aldercombe, just over the county boundary of Cornwall. Immediately after his marriage this young man carried out the first reconstruction to the building, which had remained virtually unaltered since it was built nearly six hundred years earlier. Queen Anne was on the throne of England at that time, and the new owner rebuilt the south wing of the house in the style of that period. We are reminded of this by a stone on the wall inscribed P.O. and M. (Paul Orchard and Mary) 1705.

Their son, also called Paul, carried out major alterations fifty years later. He levelled the Great Hall to the ground, pulled down the Abbey Chapel and reduced the east side of the main building to the level of the cloisters. He built three reception rooms over the latter area, with bedrooms above them, in the Georgian Gothic style, showing the influence of the Strawberry Hill design of Lord Walpole so fashionable at that time. He also constructed a library within the original walls of the Abbey on the west side, and the work was completed in 1779. Paul Orchard was for many years the Member of Parliament for Callington in Cornwall, and would undoubtedly have needed improved accommodation for the visitors he entertained in that capacity.

At Paul's death there was, again, no son to inherit the property, but his sister, Ann, eventually married George Buck of Bideford. It was their grandson, Sir George Stucley, who was the next owner to make important alterations to the Abbey. He moved there in 1845, and his changes were mainly of a decorative nature, typical of that Victorian period. The only structural change made by

Sir George was a new front hall and entrance, for which he employed the services of the eminent architect Sir George Gilbert Scott in 1862.

To walk through the house is to be transported back in history more than eight hundred years, through documents, pictures and silver, as well as by the actual building. Sir Dennis Stucley discovered in 1956 documents of great interest which had lain hidden in a chest in the basement for many years. One of the earliest of these carries the seal of Edward IV, bestowing various privileges on the monks of that time. Another document gives an account of the arrest on Plymouth Hoe of Sir Walter Raleigh, by a forebear of Sir Dennis, Sir Lewis Stucley, who later took Raleigh to the Tower of London. It seems that Raleigh had captured a Spanish ship containing a large amount of loot. He had promised half of this to Sir Lewis Stucley's father, but instead he kept the whole and was imprisoned for his greed.

Many of the paintings in the house, by well-known artists, are of generations of the family who lived at the Abbey after it became a private dwelling. The earliest of these is of the great nephew of William Abbott, to whom the Abbey was given by Henry VIII. In the same room can be seen a painting of Paul Orchard who married Mary Luttrell, the second heiress, in 1704, and who rebuilt the south wing in the Queen Anne style. These pictures are by Sir Joshua Reynolds. Two other paintings by the same artist are of the second Paul Orchard and his wife. There are other artists represented in the house, such as Thomas Gainsborough, Alan Ramsey and Thomas Hudson, tutor to Sir Joshua Reynolds. Perhaps the most lovely of all these is Hudson's 'Lady in Satin' — a type of painting at which he excelled. In the same room we find a painting of the great Victorian, Sir George Stucley, grandfather of Sir Dennis, who did so much to brighten what must have been a rather dreary dwelling.

In the drawing room there is a very good example of oak linenfold panelling. Sir George had this erected when he came to the Abbey in 1845, copied from that in the House of Lords. In this room, too, there are some very attractive murals depicting scenes in English history in which Sir George believed his forebears to have taken a part.

In the next room there is a portrait of Louisa Grenville, the second wife of Sir George, painted by Graves, a fashionable Victorian artist. This lady was a descendant of Sir Richard Grenville, the great Elizabethan, and was the grandmother of Sir Dennis. The fireplace in this room is of Maltese stone, brought by Sir George in his yacht to Hartland Quay and worked at the Abbey in 1864.

The dining room is surrounded by oak panelling erected and painted in bright Victorian colours by Sir George in 1862. This had been taken from the Great Hall of the Abbey when it was demolished a hundred years before. The pictures in this room are of historic interest, being of Sir Richard Grenville's family. There are portraits of his son, Sir Bernard, and his wife, and of his grandson, Sir Beville, who was a loyalist leader in the Civil War. The latter was killed by Cromwellian troops at the Battle of Lansdown, where a memorial to him can still be seen. His three sons are also portrayed in that room: John, Dennis and Bernard.

John, the eldest, was at the battle of Lansdown when his father was killed; after this he retreated through Devon and Cornwall to the Scilly Isles, where he subsequently contrived the restoration of the monarchy with his friend General George Monk, later the Duke of Albermarle. George Monk had a younger brother, Nicholas, who became rector of Kilkhampton, a parish quite near to Hartland. He was appointed by John Grenville, the patron of the living.

John took the unusual step of sending Nicholas all the way to Edinburgh, with an offer by the king of £100,000 per annum to General Monk if he would restore the monarchy. Nicholas, a humble parish priest, was able to do this without being suspected by Cromwell's men. He met his brother George in Edinburgh, and handed over the message. The General then marched his army all the way to London without firing a shot, met up with Charles — the deposed heir — and the monarchy was later restored. Charles created John Grenville the first Lord Bath for his services to General George Monk in achieving that end.

In the Queen Anne wing of the house, the breakfast room has panelling, door fittings and fireplace of that period. There is also a picture of Doctor William Stukely, a well-known archaeologist of the early eighteenth century, who was responsible for saving Stonehenge, Avebury and Hadrian's Wall for the nation. The first of these was being used at that time as a quarry, and Dr Stukely stirred the conscience of the nation to take the action to protect these ancient sites.